Robert Hussey

The Rise of the Papal Power

Robert Hussey

The Rise of the Papal Power

ISBN/EAN: 9783337023706

Printed in Europe, USA, Canada, Australia, Japan

Cover: Foto ©ninafisch / pixelio.de

More available books at **www.hansebooks.com**

THE RISE

OF

THE PAPAL POWER

TRACED

IN THREE LECTURES.

BY

ROBERT HUSSEY, B.D.

LATE REGIUS PROFESSOR OF ECCLESIASTICAL HISTORY.

Whoso boasteth himself of a false gift, is like clouds and wind without rain. Prov.

A NEW EDITION, WITH THE AUTHOR'S LAST ADDITIONS.

OXFORD

AT THE CLARENDON PRESS

MDCCCLXIII.

PRINTED BY

T. COMBE, M.A., E. PICKARD HALL, AND H. LATHAM, M.A.

ADVERTISEMENT.

THIS second edition of Professor Hussey's Lectures on the Rise of the Papal Power is due to the Delegates of the Clarendon Press. It is a reprint of the former edition; with such additions to the Notes as had been made by the Author in the margin of his own printed copy, and a few slight corrections of the text. The Author's additions are placed between brackets. The references have been compared and verified.

In commencing these Lectures with the Council of Sardica, A. D. 347, alleging for the Papal Power before that time only "precedence among equals willingly conceded," the Author has not embraced the whole of the subject; not in fact the actual beginning of the question of appellate

jurisdiction, as he himself intimates. See Lect. I.
p. 10. He wished to trace the steps historically
by which Rome appeared to him to have risen
beyond actual " precedence among equals," and to
arrogate to herself by little and little her claim of
absolute and divine authority. We cannot be
allowed to presume the whole issue in the phrase
" honour to the memory of Peter," which is the
ground of the Sardican Canon, any more than in
our Lord's words, "Tu es Petrus :" whether therefore the Bull " Unam Sanctam" be " virtually
contained and latent" (see Lect. III. p. 200) in
" honour to the memory of Peter," or not, it was
competent to the Author to trace the steps of this
wondrous development, that they might speak
for themselves.

The Church of England is not pledged to deny,
that it might have been agreeable to the counsel
of Christ, that His Church should have received
an organic unity : that however such unity should
have taken effect and endured, it was necessary

that it should not have been the work of "a worldly principle within the Church." See Lect. III. p. 148. To have kept the faith would not have been enough alone : seeing that it concerned the very foundations of the honour of Peter, that he should "savour the things that be of God, not the things that be of men;" (Matt. xvi. 23) that nothing resembling the ambition of the Gentiles should have place in him; (Matt. xx. 25) that he at least should not seek κατακυριεύειν τῶν κλήρων. (1 Pet. v. 3.) Alas! when most vaunting our fidelity we are nearest to a fall; when most confident in our infallibility, farthest from being converted, and farthest from strengthening our brethren.

Of the Lectures here presented to the Reader nothing more need be said. But it is intended to add a brief Memoir of the Author, with a list of his published works: and a list of Lectures still remaining in MS. is given below [a]; had he lived

---

[a] See infra, A. p. xxiii.

to select, and to prepare them himself for the press, some of them might have seen the light, especially if " the state of things" (to use his own words) "had seemed to call for them."

Robert Hussey was the fourth son, and the tenth among twelve children [b], of the Rev. William Hussey, for forty-nine years Rector of Sandhurst in Kent. He was born October 7, 1801. He learned his letters from the tombstones in the church-yard, by the help of his nurse; so that, when it was thought to be time that he should begin with his alphabet, it was found that he had stolen a march upon his teachers. His next instructress was an elder sister: but the early morning only was given to lessons. Honest and singleminded herself, she thoroughly appreciated the eager, energetic, and truthful child she had the teaching

---

[b] The eldest of this family is known in Oxford, as Mrs. Sutherland, by her gift to the Bodleian Library of Prints in illustration of Clarendon's History, &c.

of: and whatever Robert did he did heartily. He was always persevering and undaunted in what he undertook, even after repeated failures. Such is the tradition of the family: and the recollections of those who knew him in after years respond well to this beginning.

The boys of the family were allowed much liberty, subject to an acknowledged law among themselves, which stood in the place of supervision and closer confinement: thus Robert Hussey led a healthy out-of-door life, addicted more to fishing than other amusements; but it was a life more calculated to promote physical training, than to enable him to take at once a high place at school.

For a time he was at the Grammar-School of Rochester, under the care of Dr. Griffiths; but in 1814 he was sent to Westminster School, and in 1816 became a King's Scholar in S. Peter's College. He was the seventh elected; a position which was no omen of his future distinctions.

He was at that time tall, and in appearance athletic, and was soon taken into the college boat; too soon perchance, for at this time he suffered from a long and severe illness: however his recovery seemed to be complete; and he continued to cherish in himself and others a respect for manly sports. As a scholar, he made steady and uniform progress.

In 1821 he was elected to a Studentship of Christ Church, and became a pupil of the Rev. John Bull. The same qualities of body and of mind still shaped his course: he rowed in the Christ Church boat, and he came out in the First Class, both in Classics and Mathematics. On the 14th of January 1825, he took the degree of B. A., and was immediately engaged in tuition.

He was now employed by Professor Gaisford, to prepare for the University Press that edition of Homer's Odyssey which was published at Oxford in 1827: and he used to count himself fortunate in having thus early undergone the discipline of exactness due to literary work. A further advantage he owed to Dr. Gaisford, who in the mean time had become Dean of Christ Church, when in his person the Dean revived the long neglected duties of the Greek Lectureship in Christ Church: and he lectured on Greek and Latin Scholarship until he became Censor. About this time he offered himself as a candidate for the Head Mastership of Harrow School, when the Rev. Christopher Wordsworth was appointed.

His first published work was an Essay on the Ancient Weights and Money, which came out in 1836. For this purpose he had combined his long-vacation rambles with a diligent examination of the ancient coins in different museums at home and abroad.

In the same year he served the office of Proctor: and it was after consultation with the Proctors of that year, that the Vice-Chancellor, Dr. Gilbert, revived the Latin celebration of Holy Communion before the beginning of each University Term.

At the expiration of his year of office he proceeded to the degree of B. D.

In 1838 he was appointed one of the Public Examiners; and whilst in this office he published his earlier educational tracts.

He took a lively interest in the discussions of the Ashmolean Society: but of his part in them only one paper exists in print, viz. an Account of the Roman Road from Alchester to Dorchester[c]; there exists also one in manuscript on the Growth of the Flea.

He had already (in 1831) been appointed one of the Select Preachers before the University; now (in 1841) the Bishop of London, as Dean of the Chapel Royal, appointed him one of the Preachers at Whitehall: thus, during the two years of this appointment, his ordinary occupations going on as usual, he preached on Sundays in the alternate months at Whitehall. The journey from Oxford to London was still made by coach, and his health

[c] Printed for the Ashmolean Society.

was no longer what it had been: he felt the pressure, and thought at first to find a remedy in early morning exercise, though he probably required indulgence and rest.

Relief came however in a form not expected. In 1842 Sir R. Peel recommended him to the Queen for the Regius Professorship of Ecclesiastical History, which the University proposed to endow with a stipend, till the Canonry of Christ Church, already secured to it by Act of Parliament, should become vacant. Then he relinquished his college duties; and in 1843 his duties at Whitehall expired. His subsequent labours however would seem rest to few, but they were rest to him; for he was, more than ever he had been since the days of boyhood, master of his own time: and the change itself to new and congenial studies was an appreciable benefit.

He commenced the duties of his Professorship by reading with his class the text of the earlier Ecclesiastical Historians; once a week, or oftener, delivering in public the Lectures of which mention has been made. That the first Professor should begin with the works which make the foundation of the history of the Christian Church was but fitting; but he may be supposed to have been this way inclined by his early study of these works in attendance upon the Lectures of Professor Burton; whilst the long habit of tuition inclined him to the catechetical method. He next read, in the same way, the text of the History of the venerable Bede. He was thus led immediately, by the want of manuals, to print the texts of his authors in more convenient editions.

He also read with his class the History of the Reformation from Collier.

The class-books having been furnished, he proceeded with critical editions of Socrates and Sozomen: the latter was in the press at the time of his death.

He was not one to have been unaffected by the deep stirring of the religious mind, which was going on during the thirty years of his University career; still less one to have carried his stronger emotions on the surface : many owe to his deliberate convictions, under God's grace, the stay and current of their lives. No man was less addicted to the narrow spirit of party, or gave more dutiful and temperate consideration to the many questions, academical and ecclesiastical, which arose in his time. He was many times called on to exercise his vote, and was never backward to express an opinion on the exciting subjects of the day; always anxious lest the constitutional law of the University should be overborne in the prevalence of temporary interests. Some of his printed tracts bear on such points.

Other tracts show how early he had given his thoughts to matters which have since thriven or lingered in other hands. I may mention, a system of Professorial teaching; the Education of the Middle Classes; the importance of a more elaborate Elocution on the part of the Clergy;

the advantage of a wider study of Music in the University.

When he gave up his office of Censor in Christ Church, he received a parting Memorial from his pupils and others, 'Egregiam in eo mirati æquitatem:' a brief testimony; but it was that singular equity of purpose, and tried uprightness, which gave strength to his well considered opinion, as well as inspiring confidence in those placed under his care.

In 1845 he was presented by the Dean and Chapter of Christ Church to the Perpetual Curacy of Binsey, a small parish within a walk of Oxford. It gave him pastoral duties, and led to his being appointed Rural Dean by Bishop Wilberforce; and subsequently elected one of the Proctors to represent the Clergy of the Diocese of Oxford in Convocation.

In the same year he married Elizabeth, the second daughter of the Rev. Jacob Ley, Rector of Ashprington, in the county of Devon; by whom he had one daughter, born in 1852.

He was now residing in Beaumont Street in Oxford, with the cure of Binsey and the duties of a Professor. Almost from the first he found it expedient to preach at Binsey from short notes, where the congregation was both very small and very far from learned: his parochial visits were made with the same regularity which he practised in other things.

However, in 1846, he was appointed a second time Select Preacher before the University; being also called upon to preach in his turn as a Theological Professor. His first published Sermon had been printed at the request of the younger members of Christ Church, who were present on Easter day, 1841: and in 1849 was published a volume of Sermons, mostly Academical. Other single Sermons have been published by request. They were generally heard with marked attention; but they have scarcely obtained a corresponding place in popular estimation : one however, the last published, which was an Ordination Sermon, deserves throughout a careful study.

The Preface to the printed volume, drawn forth by the theory founded upon the Syrian Fragments of the Epistles of S. Ignatius, is a good specimen of his critical and argumentative power.

In 1854 was passed the Act of Parliament for reforming the University : Professor Hussey's evidence upon the recommendations of Her Majesty's Commissioners for inquiring into the state of the University of Oxford, will be found in the Report and Evidence (pp. 219–248) printed at the University Press, 1853.

On the fifteenth day of Michaelmas Term, Professor Hussey was chosen one of the Professorial Members of the Hebdomadal Council; and chosen by so great a concurrence of votes, as to have been generally noticeable, and no small surprise to himself. And he proved an industrious and valuable

Member of the Council, at a time when the body of the University Statutes were to be revised in accordance with the parliamentary provisions.

Another subject especially engaged his attention, namely, the decreasing study of Theology; it gave him real concern: it was the subject of his last Sermon[d] before the University; and the occasion of a proposition made by him in the Hebdomadal Council on Monday, December 1, 1856, for the special consideration of the subject, and for the appointment of a Committee. He returned from the Council weary, having felt and exhibited more than his usual interest in the proceedings; passed the evening at home; and retired early, saying, that he wanted rest, but that he must be at the meeting of the Council on the morrow. And rest came, — rest, after which is no more labour. No one knew better than he how near at hand that rest might be at

[d] On Sunday, October 12.

any time. Little incidents, scarcely noticed when they occurred, brought to mind afterwards, to those who had witnessed them, how present to him was the likelihood of an early removal and short warning. His accounts were written up to the last moment: never had executors greater quietness.

In other ways he seemed to be gathering himself up for the business which he had taken in hand; not with any presentiment of immediate danger, but from the feeling that all his strength was due, and would be needed for it: therefore on the evening of Sunday he had prepared his notes of a Sermon for the Sunday following, which was usually with him an engagement at home on Friday, saying, that he should be very much occupied the next week with business, which would require much thought and his best. consideration. On the Monday evening he executed the conveyance of the site of the Parochial School at Sandford, and with it posted a letter to the

Bishop of Oxford, requesting him to accept his resignation of Binsey.

Faintings, not unfrequent, had betrayed to his medical friends the feeble action of the heart. On the morning of the 2nd of December, when he would have risen, another such fainting occurred; but he recovered sufficiently to dictate a note of excuse to the Vice-Chancellor for his absence from the Council. He appeared to revive, and to be pleased to have his child at play in his room; but could not bear to have her placed upon his bed, as had been his wont in some former indispositions: but early in the afternoon a second failure of the heart ensued; and there was no recovery.

He did not live to be Canon of Christ Church, of which Canonry he held the Queen's Letters Patent: if it had been otherwise, his dust might have mingled with that of many who had been instructors and friends. He was buried at the east end of the church of Sandford on Thames; in which parish he had a few years before acquired

c

land by purchase from the Duke of Marl-borough.

To his widow he bequeathed the copyright in his works; those at least which were not under-taken for the Delegates of the University Press; [e] also his unpublished papers. To the Dean and Chapter of Christ Church he bequeathed so much of his library as related to Ecclesiastical History and Patristic Theology, for the use of his successor in the Chair.

STAVERTON, *October* 31, 1863.

[e] See infra, B. p. xxvi.

A.

LIST OF LECTURES REMAINING IN MS.

Opening Lecture, Michaelmas Term, 1842 ; with additions, 1852.

Introduction to Eusebius (1842); revised 1846.

Chronology (1842) ; revised 1844.

Philo Judæus, 1842.

Patres Apostolici (1842); revised 1849.

Early Persecutions, 1842.

Apologists, 1842.

Jewish War, 1843.

Easter Question, Hilary Term, 1843.

Heresies, i. 1843.

Heresies, ii. 1843.

Heresies, iii. 1843.

Heresies, iv. 1843.   Novatians and Donatists.

Propagation of the Gospel, 1843.

Council of Nice, Easter Term, 1843.

St. Basil, 1843.

Nestorius and Eutyches, 1843.

Monks, 1843.

Western Church, 1843 ; with Supplement to Socrates, 1851.

Socrates.   Life of Constantine, 1844.

Two Lectures on Council of Ephesus, Michaelmas Term, 1843.

Councils of Constantinople and Ephesus ii, 1843.

Council of Chalcedon, 1843.

Council of Constantinople ii, 1843.

Council of Constantinople iii, 1843.

Council Quinisextum, Hilary Term, 1844.

Council of Nice ii, 1844.   Iconoclasts.

Council of Constantinople iv, 1844.

Council of Lateran i, 1844.   Division of Eastern and Western Churches.

Councils of Lateran ii, iii, iv, 1844.

Councils of Lyons i, ii, 1844.

Pelasgians i, Act Term, 1844.

Pelasgians ii, 1844.

Semi-Pelagians, Michaelmas Term, 1844.

Early Commentators, Act Term, 1848.

Two Lectures on the Three Creeds, Hilary Term, 1853.

The Three Orders of the Ministry, Michaelmas Term, 1853.

Origin of Councils, Michaelmas Term, 1854.

Anglo-Saxon Church, Easter Term, 1845.

Influence of Rome in England, 1846.   Causes of the Reformation.

Influence of Rome, A. D. 1072–1186, 1846.

Influence of Rome to 1196, 1847.   Disputes of the Monks at Canterbury.

Influence of Rome, 1847.   King John.

Influence of Rome to 1253, 1847.

Eighteen Lectures on the History of the Reformation, 1854–6.

Three Lectures on the Rise of the Papal Power, Hilary Term, 1849 –50, were published in 1851. (These Lectures had their place between the 4th and 5th of the series of Hilary Term, 1844.)

B.

LIST OF PUBLISHED WORKS.

An Essay on the Ancient Weights and Money, and the Roman and Greek Liquid Measures; with an Appendix on the Roman and Greek Foot. By the Rev. ROBERT HUSSEY, M.A., Student of Christ Church. *Oxford*, 1836.

An Examination of the New Form of the Statutes Tit. IV. Tit. V.; with Hints for establishing a System of Professorial Teaching. By ROBERT HUSSEY, B.D., Censor of Christ Church. (A letter to the Rev. A.T. GILBERT, D.D., Vice-Chancellor of the University). *Oxford*, 1839.

A Letter to Thomas Dyke Acland, Esq., M.P., on the System of Education to be established in the Diocesan Schools for the Middle Classes. By the Rev. ROBERT HUSSEY, B.D., Student of Christ Church, Oxford. *London*, 1839.

A Help to Young Clergymen in Reading and Preaching in the Congregation of the Church. By PRESBYTERUS. *Oxford*, 1839.

An Account of the Roman Road from Alchester to Dorchester, and other Roman Remains in the Neighbourhood: being the substance of a Paper read to the Ashmolean Society, Nov. 9, 1840. By the Rev. ROBERT HUSSEY, B.D., Student of Christ Church, Oxford. (For the Ashmolean Society.) 1841.

The Great Contest. A Sermon preached in the Cathedral of Christ Church, on Easter-Day, April 11, 1841. By ROBERT HUSSEY, B.D., Censor of Christ Church. (Published by request). *Oxford*, 1841.

Socratis Scholastici Historiæ Ecclesiasticæ Libri Septem. Ex recensione H. Valesii. *Oxonii, e Typographeo Academico*, 1844.

Evagrii Scholastici Epiphaniensis et ex Præfectis Ecclesiasticæ Historiæ Libri Sex. Ex recensione H. Valesii.
Oxonii, e Typographeo Academico, 1844.

Reasons for Voting upon the Third Question to be proposed in Convocation on the 13th inst. (February). By ROBERT HUS-SEY, B. D., Regius Professor of Ecclesiastical History.
Oxford, 1845.

Bedæ Historia Ecclesiastica Gentis Anglorum. Cum opusculis quibusdam et Epistola Bonifacii ad Cudbertum Archiepiscopum. Cura ROBERTI HUSSEY, B. D., Histor. Ecclesiast. Prof. Reg. *Oxonii, e Typographeo Academico*, 1846.

The Church from the Beginning until Now. A Sermon preached at St. Mary's in Oxford, October 31, 1847, before the University. By ROBERT HUSSEY, B. D., Regius Professor of Ecclesiastical History. (Published by request.) *Oxford*, 1847.

Remarks on some Proposed Changes in the Public Examinations. By ROBERT HUSSEY, B. D., Regius Professor of Ecclesiastical History. *Oxford*, 1848.

A Letter to the Rev. the Vice-Chancellor, on the proposed Three Examinations. By ROBERT HUSSEY, B. D., Regius Professor of Ecclesiastical History, and late Censor of Christ Church.
Oxford, 1849.

Sermons, mostly Academical: with a Preface containing a refutation of the theory founded upon the Syriac Fragments of the Epistles of St. Ignatius. By ROBERT HUSSEY, B. D., Regius Professor of Ecclesiastical History; late Censor of Christ Church, and Whitehall Preacher. *Oxford*, 1849.

The Rise of the Papal Power traced, in Three Lectures. By ROBERT HUSSEY, B.D., Regius Professor of Ecclesiastical History. *Oxford,* 1851.

Socratis Scholastici Ecclesiastica Historia. Edidit ROBERTUS HUSSEY, S. T. B., Historiæ Ecclesiasticæ Professor Regius. Tomi iii. *Oxonii, e Typographeo Academico,* 1853.

University Prospects and University Duties. A Sermon preached at St. Mary's Church, before the University of Oxford, October 15, 1854. *Oxford,* 1854.

The Atonement of our Lord Jesus Christ. A Sermon preached at the Ordination holden by the Bishop of Oxford in Christ Church Cathedral, December 23, 1855, and published by request. By ROBERT HUSSEY, B. D., Regius Professor of Ecclesiastical History, Perpetual Curate of Binsey, and Rural Dean of Oxford. *Oxford,* 1856.

Sozomeni Ecclesiastica Historia. Edidit ROBERTUS HUSSEY, S. T. B., nuper Historiæ Ecclesiasticæ Professor Regius. Tomi iii. *Oxonii, e Typographeo Academico,* 1860.

N. B. This work was in the press at the time of Professor Hussey's decease, and was completed for the Delegates of the University Press by the Rev. John Barrow, D.D., late Principal of St. Edmund's Hall ; who has prefixed an Advertisement to the Reader, exactly describing the state of forwardness in which he found the edition.

PREFACE.

THESE Lectures, originally written (with no thought of publishing) for the Students in Ecclesiastical History, and read in the Course of Lectures to my Class, are now published with some additional matter; under the idea, that in the present state of things, they might be useful for the information of readers who have little opportunity to examine original authors for themselves, upon the real nature of the Roman claim of Supremacy.

Many of those doctrines and practices of the Roman Communion, to which we object, are so explained away, that to the minds of those who receive them, they become different things from what they appear to those who protest against them. *The Papal Supremacy* is not so: *that* is an *Historical Fact,* which cannot be explained away:

for it is written in the annals of the civilized world, in characters to be read alike by all eyes.

And the *Supremacy* is the essence of the whole Roman system. Take away the assertion of S. Peter's Supremacy and the Pope's equal power as his successor, and the Roman Church is *Roman* and *imperial* no longer: it is then no more to the rest of Christendom than the Church of Ethiopia or Armenia would be, except so far as one branch might be more pure, enlightened, or efficient than another.

As a *doctrine* too, the belief in the Supremacy is the fundamental article of all belief. For everything believed in that system must be believed with implicit obedience to the divine authority of S. Peter's successor; or else it is not held as the true doctrine of the system: and, *" to be separate from S. Peter* (that is, from the Roman obedience) *is to be separate from Christ* [a]*."*

[a] Hoc enim jurare (not to appeal to Rome) beatum Petrum est abjurare. *Qui autem beatum Petrum abjurat, Christum qui eum super Ecclesiam suam Principem fecit, indubitanter abjurat,* said Anselm. See Eadmer, Hist. Nov. ii. p. 48. ed. Gerb. That holy and noble-minded man had but too much reason to appeal

Thus this dogma, which was originally no part of Christ's religion, but really only a "development" of the question, "*which should be the greatest among the disciples* [b] *?*" has been made into a doctrine necessary for salvation, and the condition without which the Roman Communion offers no hope of life.

But "*Peter and James and John, after the Ascension of the Saviour, did not put in any claim for rank, on the ground that they also had been highly honoured by the Lord, but they elected James the Just to be Bishop of Jerusalem,*" says a writer at the end of the second century[c]. Which true

to *any* ecclesiastical tribunal against the tyrant William Rufus : but neither his virtues nor the hardship of his case can make a false doctrine to be true. Pope Paschal II. countenanced the doctrine, when he pronounced sentence of *excommunication* in the words, "We exclude *from the grace of S. Peter and our fellowship*," (a beati Petri gratia, et a nostra societate excludimus.) Ibid. iii. p. 66, and Mansi, xx. c. 982. And Bonifacius VIII. asserted it fully and peremptorily in the Bull "Unam Sanctam." See below, p. 179.

b Mark ix. 33, Luke ix. 46.

c " Πέτρον γάρ," φησι, " καὶ Ἰάκωβον καὶ Ἰωάννην μετὰ τὴν ἀνάληψιν τοῦ Σωτῆρος, ὡς ἂν καὶ ὑπὸ τοῦ Κυρίου προτετιμημένους, μὴ ἐπιδικάζεσθαι δόξης, ἀλλ' Ἰάκωβον τὸν δίκαιον ἐπίσκοπον Ἱεροσο-

statement of facts, while it is alone conclusive against the idea of the divinely-bestowed Supremacy of S. Peter, in the time of the Apostles, expresses also the sentiment of the Church on that point, in the age of the writer, shewing that no such thing was acknowledged by the Church then.

The writers of the first three centuries do not recognise any such Supremacy belonging to Rome. They do not speak on the point in such terms as they must have spoken if they had held the same doctrine of the Supremacy which was held in later ages; and in all their strong expressions of honour to the Roman See, they *just omit* that very point which a " Papal" writer would have been careful to put first of all, the essence of the Supremacy, the *government* of the Church by *divine authority*.

If Irenæus or Tertullian had held the same

λύμων ἐλέσθαι." Euseb. Hist. Eccl. ii. i. from the sixth book of the Hypotyposes of Clemens of Alexandria. We might add, that Eusebius' citation of this passage is also evidence that he himself did not know of any Supremacy of S. Peter and his successors in the beginning of the fourth century.

doctrine on this point as Ennodius of Pavia [d] or Henry Kalteisen [e], they could not but have expressed it, when they had occasion to speak of Rome as they have spoken. And how could S. Ignatius have written an Epistle to the Roman Church, as he did, without naming the Pope, nor alluding to his authority, if such doctrines had been held by the Church in his time?

The history of the Papal Supremacy is a complete refutation of it. Seeing *when*, and *how*, it became what *it is*, we perceive what it *originally was not;* and thence what it *never ought to have been.*

Is it credible that an Institution of our blessed Lord, of such vital moment to His whole Church, as this Supremacy would have been if it were His command, should have been unknown to the Church for so long, denied as soon as declared, and always resisted by a great part of the Church? Is it credible that such men as S. Basil [f], S. Chry-

---

[d] See p. 124.

[e] See p. 196.

[f] The argument of Pope Gregory IX. against Germanus, the

sostom, S. Cyprian, Theodoret, and the Eastern and African Churches generally, should have been so ignorant of the true doctrine of the Church, as not to know that our Lord committed to the Bishop of Rome the absolute government of the Church, (and that too a doctrine necessary for salvation) if the Church had ever received such a command from Him? Is it credible that, if it were a divine ordinance, in force from primitive times, we should be able to point out with cer-

---

Patriarch of Constantinople, is a fallacy, or rather he states only half the case, when he compares the great Fathers of the Greek Church to the Prophets who were left in the kingdom of Samaria : " Quod Chrysostomus, Nazianzenus, et magnus Basilius, et Cyrillus emicuerint in cœtu dissentientium, eadem fuit cœlestis altitudo consilii, qua degere voluit inter idololatras Eliam et Elisæum, et filios prophetarum." Mansi, xxiii. c. 59. To make the cases parallel he ought to have shewn, that the *true Prophets* not only lived among the idolaters of Israel, but also *countenanced their idolatry.* But they lived among them to *bear witness against them :* the Greek Fathers, on the contrary, countenanced and abetted the Greek Church in asserting their independence, which was *their "idolatry,"* the *"disobedience"* to Rome. [καὶ οὐχ ὅτι ἀποστολικός ἐστι θρόνος ᾐδέσθησαν οὔθ᾽ ὅτι μητρόπολις ἡ ῾Ρώμη τῆς ῾Ρωμανίας ἐστὶν εὐλαβήθησαν, says Athanasius of the Arians' conduct to P. Liberius, Hist. Ar. ad Mont. 35 : not a word of the divine right.]

tainty *where* in the history of the Church it first begins, and to trace, as we can trace it, every step of the progress of it? That we should have to confess, as, alas! we must confess, if we would speak the truth of history, that it grew up and increased by means of usurpations and frequent acts of oppression, favoured by the weakness of other parts of the Church and the vices of ages, often contrary to Christian charity and to rights.

This is not possible. Its own history overthrows it. And the design of the following Memoir is to present such a faithful picture of the authentic acts and proceedings by which it arose and advanced, that to impartial minds THE FACTS MAY SPEAK, FOR THEMSELVES.

The facts *do* speak with the voice of truth, which nothing will ever silence, against the system of the Roman Communion, as it now is. It is no pleasure to me, God knows, to dip my pen in gall, and rail at " Antichristian corrup-

ᵍ [There are many arguments against S. Peter's being " Head of the Church" in J. Hus. de Eccles. ix. Hus. Op. i. p. 260, &c. Also Contr. Stanislaum, c. iv.–vi. p. 344–350.] ed. Norimb. 1715.

tions," or the faults of any community " that nameth the name of Christ." And, in these times of doubt and fear especially, every good man would rather labour to " *build up*," than to " *pull down*." But something we have a right to say in our own defence, against those who *deny that we possess anything*, and would take from us everything which we have, *if the power were given them.*

And it is right too that people should know what the Roman claims are : so that neither members of our own Communion, nor any other, should draw comparisons and attempt to strike a balance, while the actual pretensions of Rome, and the real nature and extent of what she claims as her right, are kept out of sight, or unknown. Where these things are not known, or apprehended but vaguely and indefinitely, *imagined* rather than *known,* it is not surprising that prepossessions should be excited in favour of that from which religious minds would recoil, if they had seen the naked truth. For it is a principle of our nature, and one which it is easy to act upon,. that, *omne ignotum pro magnifico.*

But no circumstances can make falsehood, or that which is founded on falsehood, to be truth. No difficulties, perplexities, alarm, or dissatisfaction which men may feel in that branch of the Church of Christ in which the providence of God has placed them, can justify them before God in embracing a system founded on a false principle. If there be any among us who have ever thought of adopting the Roman system, surely they are bound, under a fearful responsibility, to look narrowly, and see, *to what* that system pledges them, and whether they are prepared to affirm what that system affirms concerning the Pope, and to maintain that the *whole doctrine of the Supremacy,* with *all that it has ever asserted, claimed,* or *done,* is *Divine Truth,* and the *Ordinance of Christ.* Let them then read the history of the Supremacy: and judge candidly whether indeed " this thing be of God" or " of man."

The Roman claim places the whole Church in

a "*false position;*" and it can hardly be believed that the battle of the Church against the world is to be fought under such a "Head." If the Roman Church does the Lord's work, it must be just so far as she is *not Roman, not* "above" all other Churches; but so far as she in conjunction with all other Churches "*holdeth the Head*[h]." And "*the branches*" all over the world must live by the sap of life which they draw from "*the Vine*" itself, from the *root;* not from the hollow trunk of a feigned Supremacy.

While Rome was the metropolis of the Roman empire, it might have been imagined perhaps that even if "S. Peter's authority" had been exaggerated a little beyond rightful truth, it could be borne with, for the sake of the great advantage accruing to the Church from the having one efficient centre of operations. But *now* this phantom, magnificent as it once might have seemed to some minds, has vanished : and the Roman Supremacy, under all the varieties of nation, man-

h Coloss. ii. 19.

ners, laws, and language, could produce nothing but *disunion* and *disorder;* while nevertheless it pretends elaborately to preserve universal agreement in one point, namely, in outward worship, by the use of a *language* which is *unintelligible to all nations alike.*

The history of the Supremacy seems also to exhibit another point in a clear light ; viz. that the Papal authority is a *political principle,* as well as a religious one. And therefore the exercise of it cannot be asked for as due to the rights of conscience, wherever the law allows " liberty of conscience." Subjects of a free government may hold what opinion they like of the Pope's authority as S. Peter's successor, and worship God as they like, without fear of molestation, while they do not disturb the public order. They would be punishable indeed *upon their own principles :* and if the relative position of the parties were inverted, they would be *in duty bound by their own principles to punish us*[1]. We however do not punish nor

[1] By the Canon (3) of the Fourth Lateran (General) Council, De Hæreticis, which contains the following enactment : " *But*

disturb them.   The law allows them perfect liberty
of conscience.   But no mandate nor functionary
of the Pope can claim a right to be received and
acknowledged within this country, in consequence
of that liberty which is allowed.

If it be said, that the authority of the Pope is
part of the religious belief of Romanists, and
therefore for the relief of their consciences it ought

*let secular powers be admonished and induced, and if necessary
even compelled, whatever office they fill, that as they wish to be
reputed believers, they shall publicly make oath in defence of the
faith, that they will truly endeavour with all their power to
exterminate from the territories under their jurisdiction all whom
the Church has marked for heretics; so that henceforth when any
one is admitted to any spiritual or temporal power, he shall be held
bound to affirm this article on oath.*

*" But if any temporal Sovereign, when required and admonished
by the Church, shall have neglected to purge his dominions of this
stain of heresy, he shall be bound with the chain of excommunication
by the Metropolitan and Provincial Bishops.   And if he should
neglect to give satisfaction within a year, this shall be made known
to the Supreme Pontiff; so that from that time he* (the Pope) *himself may declare his subjects absolved from their allegiance to him,
and may offer his dominions to be taken possession of by Catholics,
who, when the heretics are exterminated, may keep them without
any question, &c."*   Mansi, xxii. c. 987.   This is the *Law of the
Papal Supremacy.*

to be allowed; the answer is, that it is their error, or their misfortune, to have made *that* an article of their religion, which is incompatible with the independence of our Church and State. They may *think* as they like about it without personal hindrance; but they have no right therefore to expect that any act, or document, purporting to come from that authority, should be permitted to appear in this country.

For the Papacy by asserting the Supremacy necessarily assumes an attitude of hostility against every Church and nation which asserts its own religious independence. It cannot lay down the latter, without disavowing the former. It could not even treat with such a nation *consistently* upon its own principles: for it must deny our Church (for instance) to be a Church at all, and therefore on the question of religion would treat us as heathens; and it cannot disclaim the doctrine of the Supremacy, that the Vicar of Christ has a paramount authority over all temporal powers; and therefore there can be no reciprocity in any treaty with those who deny the right of the Supremacy. Whatever terms might be named as conditions on which permission to exercise authority could be granted, these would be accepted as a temporary condescension only on the part of a Power which by *divine right is supreme,* and can *command all other Powers,* but needs permission from none.

Supposing that a man had an enemy, who claimed the sole possession by right of his house and everything which it contained, it would not be thought prudent to admit such an one into the house, on the faith of a promise that he did not intend to lay hands on anything, or in simple confidence that he meant no harm, because forsooth some might think it uncivil to shut the door in his face. The Papacy is such an enemy to every nation which asserts its own spiritual independence; and must continue such, so long as it maintains the doctrine of the "Supremacy" of S. Peter's successor; and therefore it cannot claim a right to be admitted, on the general principles of toleration; rather, it cannot safely be admitted. That is to say, no public act of it can be allowed to have effect, in an independent country, upon any principle of sound policy.

If the Papacy, instead of professing to *forbear from exercising*, could renounce *all right to possess* that authority which it claims in the *"Supremacy,"* that is to say, give up and abandon all that Popes have ever asserted on this head, and be really the *Papacy* no longer, the case would be different. But in the mean time, all these claims and all these assertions of authority are only in abeyance for the present; they might be put forth again at any moment, if circumstances permitted. For instance, should any future occupant of S. Peter's Chair be animated with the spirit of a Gregory VII, or a Bonifacius VIII, he could not hesitate to do what indeed it is clear, *on the principles of the Supremacy, it would be his duty to do*, to lay this kingdom under an interdict, or to depose the Sovereign from the throne, if he had the power, and could hope by these means to extirpate the *" heretical"* Church of England, or to compel the nation to " return to the Roman obedience."

CONTENTS.

LECTURE II. pp. 55—93.

LECTURE III.   PART II.   pp. 151—209.

LECTURE I.

THE Supremacy of the See of Rome began in the fourth century. Then for the first time the *precedence* [a] *among equals* willingly conceded to Rome in early ages was turned into a claim of *authority;* which was demanded on a new ground [b], and from that time never ceased to advance in pretensions, until it assumed the form of *The Supremacy,* that is, absolute dominion throughout Christendom.

Many causes contributed to this, and they operated in various ways.

---

[a] S. Cyprian urged this as an argument for the Unity of the Church, *not* for the Papal authority. De Unit. Eccles.

[b] No such claim appears to have been made on this ground, in either of *the two* cases of Papal interference, by Victor, see Euseb. Hist. Eccl. v. 24. and by Stephen, see Cyprian. Epist. lxvii. 5. ed. Lips. 1838.

B

One of the most conspicuous and strongest links by which other Churches were connected with Rome, was the appellate jurisdiction: by which Rome claimed authority, as the supreme Court of Appeal in all ecclesiastical causes.

The origin of this may be distinctly traced to the Council of Sardica, A. D. 347. The principle having been once formally asserted there, was speedily carried out and enlarged by the language and acts of succeeding Popes.

A Council had been called to Sardica, by the joint command of the two Emperors Constantine and Constans, with the intention that it should be a General Council: but they were disappointed of their wish; for while the Western Bishops assembled there to the number of about 170, the Oriental Bishops, among whom were the Arian party, retired to Philippopolis, and formed a Synod of their own there, mustering about 80. Many things were determined at Sardica in favour of the orthodox faith, and against the Arians, as Socrates has related [c] : and moreover, which

[c] Socrat. H. E. ii. 20.

Socrates does not mention[d], the Council made twenty-one Canons.

In these Canons an appellate jurisdiction is given to the Bishop of Rome. In the third Canon[e] it is said, that "if any Bishop thought

[d] Perhaps Socrates purposely omitted mentioning these Canons, because the Greek Church never received them.

[e] Mansi, iii. c. 23. from Dionysius Exiguus' Version. In the Greek thus: ἐὰν ἔν τινι ἐπαρχίᾳ ἐπισκόπων τις ἀντικρὺς ἀδελφοῦ ἑαυτοῦ καὶ συνεπισκόπων πρᾶγμα σχοίη, μηδέτερον ἐκ τούτων ἀπὸ ἑτέρας ἐπαρχίας ἐπισκόπους ἐπιγνώμονας ἐπικαλεῖσθαι· εἰ δὲ ἄρά τις ἐπισκόπων ἔν τινι πράγματι δόξῃ κατακρίνεσθαι, καὶ ὑπολαμβάνει ἑαυτὸν μὴ σαθρὸν ἀλλὰ καλὸν ἔχειν τὸ πρᾶγμα, ἵνα καὶ αὖθις ἡ κρίσις ἀνανεωθῇ, εἰ δοκεῖ ὑμῶν τῇ ἀγάπῃ, Πέτρου τοῦ ἀποστόλου τὴν μνήμην τιμήσωμεν, καὶ γραφῆναι περὶ τούτων τῶν κρινάντων Ἰουλίῳ τῷ ἐπισκόπῳ Ῥώμης, ὥστε διὰ τῶν γειτνιώντων τῇ ἐπαρχίᾳ ἐπισκόπων, εἰ δέοι, ἀνανεωθῆναι τὸ δικαστήριον, καὶ ἐπιγνώμονας αὐτὸς παράσχοι. εἰ δὲ μὴ συστῆναι δυνάται τοιοῦτον αὐτῷ εἶναι τὸ πρᾶγμα, ὡς παλινδικίας χρῄζειν, τὰ ἅπαξ κεκριμένα μὴ ἀναλύεσθαι, τὰ δὲ ὄντα, βέβαια τυγχάνειν. "If in any province any Bishop have a cause against his brother and fellow Bishops, neither of them shall appeal to Bishops from another province to take cognizance [of it]. But if then any Bishop shall be condemned in any cause, and he think that he has not a weak but a sound cause so that also a new judgment may be had [upon it], if it please your Piety let us honour the memory of the Apostle Peter, and notice in writing concerning those who have tried [the cause] be sent to Julius the Bishop of Rome, so that, if necessary, a fresh court may be opened, [new trial be had] by Bishops near

he had good reason" to appeal from a provincial judgment of his case, and to desire a new trial, " let us, if you please, honour the memory of the Apostle Peter," and he should write to Julius the Bishop of Rome ; and the Bishop of Rome, if he thought fit, should order the case to be tried, and name judges to try it. Other clauses followed, bearing on the same point, viz. that [f] if a deposed Bishop gave notice of appeal to Rome, his place should not be filled up, until the Bishop of Rome had given sentence (Can. 4): and, that when the [g] Bishop of Rome had received an appeal, he might order the case to be tried again by the provincial Bishops, or send Legates to try the case (Can. 5): the object of which Canon was, according to Balsamon, to prevent the necessity of a journey to Rome on every appeal.

to the province, and he [Julius] may appoint judges. But if it cannot be proved that his cause is such as to require re-hearing, the first decision is not to be questioned, but what has been done is to stand good." Bevereg. Synodic. i. p. 485.

[f] Bevereg. p. 487.

[g] Bevereg. p. 488.

The effect of the whole was, that Rome had now a Canonical authority, viz. the Canons of this Council, to receive and try appeals of Bishops who wished to appeal from the decisions of Synods : but *not* authority to evoke causes to Rome, *nor* to summon Bishops *ex officio*, *nor* to proceed to review and set aside the judgments of Councils. Such a power is plainly denied by these Canons; for, by defining the power which they give to the Pope, they exclude his pretensions to a much wider power. The power which they give relates only to appeals which may be made to him.

The Greek Canonists, Balsamon and Zonaras, however maintain, that not even this power was by the Canons of Sardica given absolutely and universally to the Pope : but only over those Churches which were under Rome; and that the Patriarch of Constantinople had equal power within his own provinces [h].

That this power of the Pope, to receive and try all appeals, was not then considered an in-

[h] On Can. v. Bevereg. p. 489.

herent right belonging to his person or his see, is plain from the language of Pope Julius on the subject. For in a letter, written a few years before, to defend himself from the accusations of the Arians[i], that he had irregularly reversed their decisions, when appealed to, he no where claims this right; but argues the point on the general grounds of equity, and the evidence in the cases before him: he contends that wrong had been done, because the Arian party had not brought the question before the Church at large; "judgment ought to have been given according to the Canon of the Church, and not so as you gave it: you ought to have written to all of us, that so we might all have decided what was just:" and then he adds, that they ought especially to have written to him in a matter concerning Alexandria; alluding apparently to the connection which S. Mark, the founder of the Alexandrian Church, had with Rome; and says,

---

[i] Jul. Epist. ad Orientales in Athanas. Apolog. c. Arian. 21, 35. and Mansi, ii. c. 1211, 1229.

" Did you not know it was an old custom to write to us first, and thus that it should be decided from hence what was just?" This is all that Julius stated concerning the authority of the See of Rome in the question: shewing clearly that he knew of no right, divine or human, belonging to the Pope, of supreme jurisdiction over the rest of the Church; but only the custom of precedence and priority of place, which was always willingly conceded, and would be so still, if nothing more had been claimed.

Indeed the very fact that it was now decreed by a Canon, that appeals might be made to Rome, proves that there was no primitive rule or custom to that effect, still less a divine right belonging to the succession of S. Peter; for then the Canon would have been superfluous[k]. And moreover,

---

[k] Socrates' expression might be alleged as seeming to contradict this, κανόνος ἐκκλησιαστικοῦ κελεύοντος μὴ δεῖν παρὰ τὴν γνώμην τοῦ ἐπισκόπου Ῥώμης τὰς ἐκκλησίας κανονίζειν, " an ecclesiastical Canon decrees, that it is not right to make Canons for the Churches against the judgment of the Bishop of Rome," ii. 8. No such Canon has ever been found, nor apparently ever existed. (See Barrow, Pope's Supremacy Suppos. v. and vi.

the wording of the Canon, *let us honour the memory of the Apostle Peter*, proves that the Council acknowledged no power to govern the Church by divine right bequeathed by S. Peter to his successors.

To assert that this authority belonged to the Pope before the Canon of Sardica was made, would be virtually to set aside the authority of the Council of Sardica: but the Canons of Sardica were acknowledged at Rome, and often referred to in support of the Pope's authority.

p. 136, &c. in the Enchirid. Theol. Anti-Rom. ii. Oxford, 1852.) The Council of Antioch (A. D. 341) denied the Pope's right to rule them, μὴ δεῖν κανονίζεσθαι παρ' αὐτοῦ. Socr. ii. 15. Socrates is no great authority on such a point : and P. Julius himself does not refer to such a Canon, which he would have done if it had been what some have supposed Socrates to mean. Socrates' statement is perhaps after all nothing more than his own inference from the language in the letter of P. Julius, which has just now been quoted. Julius spoke of old custom, Socrates at once assumed the existence of a Canon, and expressed what he supposed to be the substance of it. It was however quite true, that Canons for the *whole Church* might not be made by other Churches without the concurrence of Rome, as it was true that Canons might not be made for the whole Church *by Rome* (or the Council of Sardica) without the concurrence of *all other Churches*.

The appellate jurisdiction of the Pope therefore is founded upon this Canon of Sardica.

Some indeed have said, that strictly we ought to interpret it as conveying only a personal right to Pope Julius. Certainly he is described by name in the Canon. The authority is not expressly given to the Bishop of Rome for the time being, nor to the successor of S. Peter. But the distinction, however technically just, is perhaps not important, because the precedent would have had authority, if the right had been ever admitted.

But the Council of Sardica, although named by Romanists *General* and *Œcumenical*, and collected by the Emperor's command, was not composed of the Bishops of the whole Church, and did not represent the whole Church: the Canons of it were never universally received[1]: and the par-

---

[1] The Canons of Sardica are quoted, with others in the Greek Collections, for such points as were received without objection. But these which assigned universal jurisdiction to Rome are not quoted by the Greeks, and there are many Greek Canons opposed to them. Photius says, in his Preface to the Nomocanon concerning Sardica, ἡ δὲ ἐν Σαρδικῇ καὶ ἐν Καρτα-

ticular Canons concerning the Pope's authority were always resisted by the Greek Church and the African Church. Although it is self-evident that, if it be not a divine command, (which the Canon of Sardica by its very constitution tacitly denies,) nothing less than universal consent and concurrence can be competent to impose one supreme Court of Appeal over all Ecclesiastical tribunals in the whole Church.

Perhaps one reason why the Council of Sardica made this Canon was, that the Arian or Semi-arian Council at Antioch six years before (A. D. 341) had made some Canons on the right of appealing, prohibiting all appeals beyond the Metropolitan of the province [m]; of which the object was doubtless, in part at least, to exclude

γένη, τῷ χρόνῳ τίνων τῶν λοιπῶν συνόδων προτερεύουσαι μετ᾽ αὐτὰς ἐτέθησαν διὰ τὸ πολλὰ περί τινων ἐπιχωρίων, ἤγουν τῶν δυτικῶν μέρων, διορίσασθαι. "But the Council of Sardica and that of Carthage, though earlier than some other, are put after them, because they defined many things concerning the provinces, that is, the western parts." Voelli et Justelli Bibliotheca Jur. Canonici, vol. ii. p. 795.

m Can. 14 and 15. Mansi, ii. c. 1313. Compare also Can. 6, and 12, with Athanasius' case.

the influence of Rome and the Western Church
in the question about Athanasius. The Council
of Sardica, which reversed the decisions of the
Council of Antioch, and condemned some of
the Arian leaders, might wish also to set aside
the rule which that party had made on this
point.

And another reason for making the Canon was,
their experience of the service which Rome had
often done to the Church, by defending the truth,
and sheltering those who suffered for it. Athanasius, Asclepas, Marcellus, and their friends,
had found refuge lately at Rome[n] : and Rome
at this time, and for some time afterwards, had
earned the precedence in honour always allowed
to the imperial See, not only by her martyred
Bishops and her munificence to poorer Churches,
but also by her orthodoxy, and by the courage
and ability with which she undertook the cham-
pionship of the truth against various shapes of
error. These facts may make us regret the more,
that so noble a beginning could have laid the

[n] Socrat. ii. 15, &c. Athan. Apolog. c. Arianos, 33.

foundation for a theory so erroneous and oppressive as was built upon it afterwards.

Pope Julius in this controversy uses the expression, " I declare to you what I have received from S. Peter:" and in the same sentence he had spoken of the ordinances of Paul and the traditions of the Fathers.

The Council of Sardica, in the Canon quoted, giving the judgment of appeals to the Pope, said, that appeals should be made in " honour of the memory of S. Peter."

Here is no assertion of the divine supremacy bestowed upon S. Peter, nor of the Pope's inheriting any such supremacy from S. Peter: neither is any assertion to that effect to be found (that I am aware) in this age. When S. Peter is referred to by name in the early times, in connection with the Pope, it is for a guarantee of Apostolical doctrine or discipline: not as having possessed, conveyed, or authorized to the Pope, any personal supremacy.

In later times, S. Peter's name stands for the sanction of a supreme power in the Church, supposed to be given to him by our Lord Himself, and inherited by his successors.

Liberius, who succeeded Julius in A. D. 352, must have weakened rather than increased the influence of the See by his conduct, when after having for a time boldly resisted the arguments and endured the power of the Arian Emperor Constantius, he at last sank beneath the weight of exile, and, in a moment of weakness, retracted his past judgment, and gave his assent to the acts of the Arian party[o].

Damasus, who succeeded A. D. 366, had to encounter the opposition of a competitor for the See, one Ursinus, or Ursicinus, and a disgraceful contest ensued, in which many lives were lost:

[o] Athanas. Hist. Arian. ad Mon. 41. p. 368. and Apol. c. Ar. 89. p. 204. Yet even this has been denied: so completely can party feeling blind the judgment of learned and zealous men to historical truth. See Galland. Biblioth. Patr. vol. v. p. xi. xii. As if S. Athanasius could possibly have been misinformed on this point, or could have been induced to record such an unwelcome and humiliating event by anything but the necessity of truth! It is evident, that on this point, a single statement like that of Athanasius (and he has asserted it twice) would outweigh the omission or the silence of any number of writers.

and the heathens were scandalized by such things being done in the Church of the Christians P. It was the first contest of such a kind in the history of the Papacy. Would that it had been the last!

The faction of Ursinus was condemned by a Council at Rome, and those concerned in it banished by the Emperors Gratian and Valentinian. But the Council at Rome q, (in which of course the Pope would have presided,) finding the Church still troubled by this party, appealed to the Emperors, and asked them, that, because they, the Emperors, had already given sentence in favour of Damasus, they would support his authority, and compel the provincial Bishops, in such cases as they then stated, to refer the cause to judges whom he might appoint, or to carry it to Rome if summoned by him. In this petition the Council expressly affirmed, that Damasus had submitted his own cause (in the question of the Popedom) to the Imperial Tribunal, and justified this by the example of Pope Silvester, who, they

P Ammian. Marcell. xxvii. 3.
q Mansi, iii. c. 624-627.

said, had done the same towards Constantine, and of S. Paul who appealed to Cæsar.

Gratian granted the request, and published an Imperial Edict accordingly, that persons condemned by the Pope, or any Catholic Synod, and not submitting to that judgment, should thereupon be tried by the Metropolitan of the province, or else be required to appear at Rome, if summoned, or be tried by judges whom the Pope should appoint [r].

Other circumstances a little before this contributed to increase the influence of Rome. Gratian, A. D. 378, on the death of the Arian Emperor Valens, permitted all the Bishops, whom Valens had driven into exile, to return : and in the edict to authorize this, his definition of the orthodox, whom he intended to restore, is said by Theodoret to have been "all who were in communion with Damasus [s]." The Law afterwards published, A.D. 380, 3 Kal. Mart., by Theodosius [t],

---

[r] Mansi, c. 629.

[s] Theodoret, Hist. Eccles. v. 2.

[t] Sozom. H. E. vii. 4.

at Thessalonica, in the name of Gratian, Valentinian II, and Theodosius, runs as follows: "We would have all the nations, whom our gracious government rules, to be of that religion which the divine Apostle Peter is proved to have delivered to the Romans, by the religion which even now is imparted from him, which also it is plain that the Pontiff Damasus follows, and also Peter, Bishop of Alexandria, a man of apostolical sanctity: that we may believe, according to the apostolic teaching and evangelical doctrine, in the one Godhead of the Father, Son, and Holy Ghost, of equal Majesty, in the Holy Trinity. We command that they who follow this law shall take the name of Catholic Christians: but all other foolish and insane in judgment (or, we judge) shall bear the infamy of heretical doctrine: and their meetings shall not have the name of Churches; but they shall be punished first by the Divine vengeance, afterwards by penalties from our authority, which we have received from the will of God." This stands at the beginning of the sixteenth book of the Codex Theo-

dosianus [u]. Although the name of Peter of Alexandria was thus included in the statute, little
importance seems to have been attached to it in
comparison with Rome.

When this mandate was brought to Antioch,
where there were then disputes going on about
doctrine, as well as about the possession of the
See, Damasus' orthodoxy in doctrine was much
insisted on, and they who professed to be in communion with him, were called on to shew their
agreement with him in doctrine [v].

[u] "Cunctos populos quos Clementiæ nostræ regit temperamen-
tum, in tali volumus religione versari, quam Divinum Petrum
Apostolum tradidisse Romanis, religio usque nunc ab ipso insi-
nuata declarat : quamque Pontificem Damasum sequi claret, et
Petrum Alexandriæ Episcopum, virum apostolicæ sanctitatis :
ut secundum apostolicam disciplinam, evangelicamque doctri-
nam, Patris et Filii et Spiritus Sancti unam Deitatem sub parili
Majestate et sub pia Trinitate credamus. Hanc legem sequen-
tes, Christianorum Catholicorum nomen jubemus amplecti : reli-
quos vero dementes væsanosque judicantes, hæretici dogmatis
infamiam sustinere : nec conciliabula eorum Ecclesiarum nomen
accipere, divina primum vindicta, post etiam motus nostri, quem
ex cœlesti arbitrio sumpserimus, ultione plectendos." Vol. vi.
part i. of Gothofredus' edition of the Codex Theod. xvi. i. 2. and
Clinton, Fast. Rom. A. D. 380.

[v] Theodoret, v. 3. Barrow called the letter of Damasus, Theodoret, v. 10, spurious, P. Supremacy, p. 229.

While Damasus held the See, there was much correspondence between the East and the West. The leading Bishops of the East[x] desired the advice and assistance of the West, especially of Rome, in repressing Arian and other erroneous opinions; but they found a great obstacle to this in the arrogant pretensions of the Roman Church. Instead of co-operation and union, they were met by a claim of authority, which they did not acknowledge, and could not submit to; and they complained of the haughty manner in which their judgment was rejected. They did not scruple to censure the judgment of Rome; and in addressing the Western Church, or the Pope, their style, while it was respectful and complimentary to the dignity of the parties, was at the same time the language of independence and equality. *They knew nothing of the Supremacy of Rome.*

The letter of the Eastern Bishops to the Western, after many friendly expressions, and some free suggestions, and even reproofs of decisions

---

[x] Basil defines "The East" to be "from Illyria to Egypt." Epist. lxx.

given at Rome, concludes with a request for
their assistance in the following words: "We are
not ignorant that we ought ourselves to discuss
these points, sitting together in joint deliberation
with you; but since the time does not allow it,
and delay is hurtful, (the mischief of them being
deep rooted) we were forced to send these our
brethren, that they might inform you of those
things which are omitted in this letter, and move
your Holiness to afford the much-desired help to
the Churches of God y."

S. Basil, writing to Pope Damasus himself,
asks earnestly for his help; and reminds him,
that in former times the Bishop of Rome had
given aid to other branches of the Church when
in need z : but he gives no hint of a supreme
authority, or visitatorial power of any kind, belonging to him. On the contrary, he repudiates
such a notion: "I hear," he says, "that Paulinus' party have brought letters from the West,
as if they were a warrant from some sovereign

---

y Basil, Ep. cclxiii.

z Ep. lxx. Compare his letter to Athanas. lxvi. &c.

power [a], and are proud of the documents;" but he condemned the judgment of Rome in this and other cases: he censured in strong terms the insolence of the West (Rome), which did not understand the real state of things in the East, and was too proud to learn [b]: and he seems to have alluded to P. Damasus himself, when he spoke of "a high and mighty personage seated aloft somewhere, who for that reason could not bear to hear those who from below spoke the truth to him [c]."

A little after this, another Italian [d] Synod under Ambrose, and therefore perhaps held at Milan, addressed a petition to the Emperor Theodosius,

[a] Ὥσπερ τινὸς ἀρχῆς συνθήματα. Ep. ccxvi.

[b] Ep. ccxv. ccxxxix. lxix. cxxv. cclxvi. 2. ccxiv. [P. Liberius gave Eustathius of Sebastea a letter of restitution, and he was therefore restored by Synod of Tyane, though an Arian. Basil strongly condemned this. Ep. cclxiii. 3.]

[c] He wrote, that his brother Gregory might perhaps have been a fit person to send with a deputation to the West, if he would have had to deal with "a gentleman" (ἀνδρὶ εὐγνώμονι), but not fit to meet ὑψηλῷ καὶ μετεώρῳ ἄνω που καθημένῳ, καὶ διὰ τοῦτο ἀκούειν τῶν χαμόθεν αὐτῷ τὴν ἀλήθειαν φθεγγομένων μὴ δυναμένῳ, which seems to mean the Pope. Ep. ccxv.

[d] Mansi, iii. c. 631. It seems to have been at the end of A. D. 381. The Roman editor of Damasus (Merenda, 1754) rejects this Epistle as spurious.

praying that he would not allow the Council at
Constantinople to ordain Nestorius in place of
Maximus, without first consulting Rome and the
Italian Bishops; in which they represent their
claim in these words: *Non prærogativam vindi-
camus examinis, sed consortium tamen debuit esse
communis arbitrii* [e]; "We do not claim a prior
right to judge, but yet there ought to be a concurrence in a common decision." In short, they
use the same kind of language as P. Julius used
before, not pretending to any supremacy of jurisdiction for Rome, but arguing that Rome especially ought not to be left out of any act or
deliberation of the Church at large. The opposition from Italy, which was but temporary, had
no effect upon the decision of the Council of Constantinople [f].

[e] Mansi, c. 632. See also the argument at the end of the
petition, Neque enim indignum videtur, &c. where is no hint of
a right belonging to Rome, but a parallel case is adduced, to
shew the justice of the request: which would be absurd, if Rome
had this supremacy by divine right, or by Canon: for then no
other case could be at all a parallel. [Comp. Hilar. Op. Hist.
Frag. ii. 22. v. ii. c. 640.]

[f] The letter of Damasus to Acholius, produced in the Council

S. Jerome also about this time wrote from the East to Damasus, for advice and guidance in the questions agitated about doctrine there, to ask whether he ought to confess three *"hypostases"* in the Holy Trinity; in which letter, although he professes entire confidence in the apostolic soundness of the faith of him who sat in the chair of S. Peter, the style of his address is somewhat different from that of later Romanism. He writes, *Facessat invidia. Romani culminis recedat ambitio: cum successore Piscatoris et discipulo crucis loquor. Ego nullum primum nisi Christum sequens, Beatitudini tuæ, id est, cathedræ Petri, communione consocior. Super illam Petram ædificatam Ecclesiam scio*[g], &c. "Away with jealousy. Let the ambition of Roman preeminence retire. I speak to the successor of the fisherman, and the disciple of the Cross. While

at Rome under P. Bonifacius II, A. D. 531, speaks all the contrary way, that is, against "the Cynic," (i. e. Maximus) and all in favour of the Council of Constantinople, then *about to meet.* But is this document to be trusted for genuine? N. L. See Mansi, viii. c. 749.

[g] Hieron. Epist. xv. 2. ed. Vallars.

I follow no chief but Christ, I am joined in communion with your beatitude, that is, the seat of Peter. On that rock I know the Church is built."

In A. D. 381, the second General Council was held at Constantinople, by command of the Emperor Theodosius. Two of the Canons ordained there, are a perpetual record against the Roman claim of Supremacy; the second and the third: for the second ordered, that no Bishop should invade the diocese of another, but that every episcopal province should have its own jurisdiction independent, according to the Nicene Canons: the third ordered, that the See of Constantinople should have rank next after that of Rome, because it was " *New Rome* h."

---

h The two Canons are as follows: Can. 2. Τοὺς ὑπὲρ διοίκησιν ἐπισκόπους ταῖς ὑπεροπλίοις ἐκκλησίαις μὴ ἐπιέναι, μηδὲ συγχέειν τὰς ἐκκλησίας· ἀλλὰ κατὰ τοὺς κανόνας τὸν μὲν 'Αλεξανδρείας ἐπίσκοπον τὰ ἐν Αἰγύπτῳ μόνον οἰκονομεῖν· τοὺς δὲ τῆς ἀνατολῆς ἐπισκόπους τὴν ἀνατολὴν μόνην διοικεῖν, φυλαττομένων τῶν ἐν τοῖς κανόσι τοῖς κατὰ Νικαίαν πρεσβείων τῇ 'Αντιοχέων ἐκκλησίᾳ, &c.   " Bishops beyond the bounds of any diocese shall not interfere with the Churches out of their territory, nor disturb the Churches : but according to the Canons, the Bishop of Alexandria shall manage

This Council has always been received as of authority by the Church : and it is admitted, that P. Damasus concurred in it[i], or "authorized it," as Romanists would say : and later Popes have by name acknowledged the second General Council of Constantinople. Yet when these Canons crossed their pretensions, as they always did, the Popes did not scruple to reject them, and deny their authority, even while professing to receive the authority of the Council as a General Council of the Church : as we shall see farther onwards[j].

The title *Sedes Apostolica* [k], which in later

the affairs of Egypt alone, and the Bishops of the East preside over the East alone ; but without damage to the precedence of the Church of Antioch, which is allowed by the Nicene Canons, &c." Routh. Opusc. i. p. 390. ed. 1840.

[•] Can. 3. Τὸν μέν τοι Κωνσταντινουπόλεως ἐπίσκοπον ἔχειν τὰ πρεσβεῖα τῆς τιμῆς μετὰ τὸν τῆς Ῥώμης ἐπίσκοπον, διὰ τὸ εἶναι αὐτὴν νέαν Ῥώμην. "The Bishop of Constantinople, however, shall have precedence in honour next after the Bishop of Rome, because that city is New Rome." Ibid.

[i] Non sine Damasi summi pontificis auctoritate, says Mansi, iii. c. 526.

[j] [Gregor. i. Pap. Epist. vii. 34.]

[k] See it so used by Pope Innocentius I, in his Epistle to Jerome, concerning John of Jerusalem, which was as much *sedes*

times was understood to mean Rome alone, was not so used now; but had a wider sense. In some of the disputes about authority now beginning, it was often used to distinguish the Churches which could trace their descent from an apostle [1], such as Jerusalem, Antioch, Ephesus, Rome, and Alexandria (through S. Mark). But it was also in this age applied in a still wider sense to all bishoprics, signifying the apostolic office of a Bishop. This appears in the Epistles of Paulinus of Nola, written at the end of this century [m].

During the life of P. Damasus, the Archbishop of Aragon addressed a letter [n] (doubtless Synodical) to him, asking for directions on some curious questions of Church discipline, for cases occurring in Spain. This letter reached Rome after Siricius was Pope, (A. D. 384) and he answered it in a

Apostolica as Rome, according to Pope Leo's argument against Constantinople. See Leon. Epist. lxxviii. lxxx. p. 296, 300. ed. Quesnel. fol. 1700. Compare below, p. 31, note [l].

[1] [Epist. Synod. Conc. Constant. Theodoret, H. E. v. 9. of Antioch. Sozomen, H. E. i. 17. of the four.]

[m] A.D. 394. Paulin. Epist. ad Alyp. iii. 1. p. 10. ed. Paris. 1685, [ἀποστολικὴ προεδρία, by Theodoret, H. E. iii. 19.]

[n] Mansi, iii. c. 655.

style of authority, intermixing some reproofs. His answers would stand as *Decrees* upon the several points submitted to his judgment: °indeed he speaks of the *Decreta* of his predecessor Liberius: and thus the papal Decretals grew up. P. Siricius writes here in the name of a Synod: and so all the early judgments of Rome were Synodical; although afterwards they grew into papal edicts, and passed under the name of the Pope who authorized them P.

Siricius here reminds the Spanish Archbishop, that Rome is the head of his Church, "*caput corporis tui* ᵩ."

This practice of consulting Rome was doubtless of great service to the provincial Churches in many respects for a long time. But it contributed greatly to that influence which Rome so much abused afterwards in corrupt times.

° Mansi, iii. c. 656.

P The judgments of eminent Fathers also had always an authority of like kind, τὰ παρά τινων ἁγίων πατέρων ἰδιαζόντως ἐν ἐπιστολαῖς πεύσεσί τε καὶ ἀποκρίσεσιν εὐσεβῶς εἰρημένα. Photii Praef. Nomoc. Justell. Biblioth. p. 790.

ᵩ Mansi, iii. c. 661.

ᵣ

Siricius also sent to Africa some Canons agreed to in a Synod at Rome, in such terms as meant nothing less than to impose them as a law[r].

One of these (the ninth and last) is remarkable, compared with later acts : it concerns the marriage of Clergy : and says, " Moreover we advise you, what is worthy, and modest, and honourable, that Priests and Levites should not have intercourse with their wives, because a daily necessity is laid upon them in their ministry, &c[s]."

Married Clergy were common in the African Church : and the Pope offered nothing more than his advice on the subject at present.

Siricius also decreed[t], that *the Bishop of Rome might consecrate a Bishop by himself alone.* In every other case there must be three to consecrate, by the third Canon of the Council of Nicæa.

This was a considerable stretch of power, when the Pope undertook to supersede the authority of

[r] Some others from him are given in Mansi, c. 676.

[s] Mansi, c. 669. Pope Innocentius repeated this in his Canons for the Church of Rouen. Ibid. c. 1034.

[t] Fulgent. Ferrand. Brev. Can. in Justelli, i. p. 448.

such a Canon by a rule in favour of his own See. And moreover it is *literally* condemned by an expression of P. Innocentius, when in writing about the authority of the Canons in the case of S. Chrysostom, he said, that the Church ought to follow the Canons of the Council *of Nicæa only* [u]. For although in these words he might intend chiefly to reject the second and third Canons of the Council of Constantinople [v], and probably meant to include the Canons of Sardica under the name of Nicæa, he at least asserted the authority of the Nicene Canons so strongly, that he could not consistently have allowed one of them to be completely set aside, as it was by P. Siricius' decree. And P. Leo I. asserted, that the Canons of the Council of Nicæa are unchangeable, they *" would remain to the end of the world* [x].*"* Therefore these two Popes have virtually condemned that decree of P. Siricius.

[u] Chrysost. Epist. vol. iii. p. 524. Sozom. H. E. viii. 26.

[v] Which forbad Bishops to interfere with the Church beyond their own dioceses, and asserted the dignity of the See of Constantinople. See p. 23.

[x] Leon. Ep. lxxx. 4.

About this time there was a misunderstanding
between Rome and the Oriental Church, concerning the See of Antioch. A Synod at Constantinople (A. D. 382) had recognised Flavianus
as Bishop of Antioch. Rome acknowledged Paulinus and his successor Evagrius, but not Flavianus. According to Theodoret, the Emperor at the
Pope's instance summoned Flavianus to Rome to
be tried there : but he refused to go. At last
Flavianus sent a deputation of Bishops, and peace
was made, Socrates says, in ʸDamasus' time : but
Theodoret puts it in the Popedom of Innocentius ᶻ.
It was perhaps soon after Innocentius' accession,
which was in A. D. 402.

Under Innocentius I. the influence of Rome was
greatly on the increase.

Innocentius, in his Epistle to Decentius Bishop
of Eugubium, (Gubio) which was in fact a Decretal in answer to certain questions, affirms, that
there was no Church in all Italy, Gaul, Spain,

ʸ Socr. v. 15.

ᶻ Theodoret, Hist. v. 23. ˊ Where see Valesius' notes. Comp.
Hieronym. Ep. cviii. 6. cxxvii. 7.

Africa[a], *Sicily, and the islands near, which was not founded by S. Peter or his successors:* and therefore that *all these Churches must keep all that Rome keeps,* since they all were derived from Rome[b].

This assertion, even if true, could not possibly have been proved from history in Innocentius' time: and it is in many particulars contrary to everything that history declares, or indicates as probable. But we are coming now to the period of *Papal fictions.*

To the Bishop of Rouen he sends a number of Canons or Decrees, intimating that he, the Bishop of Rouen, had asked for the Roman pattern for his authority[c]. "Romanæ ecclesiæ normam ad auctoritatem."

He sent also Canons to the Bishops of Gaul at their request[d], Decrees to Toulouse[e], and to Spain[f], (which seems to have needed some im-

---

[a] [S. Augustin speaks of "ceteris terris, unde Evangelium ad ipsam Africam venit." Epist. xliii. 3. (7.) v. ii. c. 91.]

[b] Mansi, iii. c. 1028.

[c] Ibid. c. 1032.

[d] C. 1133. This was from a Synod at Rome.

[e] C. 1038, 1066.   [f] C. 1064.

provement) to Macedonia[g], and to places in Italy[h]. And he reversed the decision of a provincial Synod in Macedonia[i]. His letter to the Bishop of Toulouse (Exuperius) is remarkable for containing a list of the books of Scripture; in which are reckoned the books of the Apocrypha, except Bel and the Dragon, and Susanna and the Elders[k].

In his correspondence with Antioch he claimed particular connection with that See, because S. Peter had once held it, before he came to Rome[l]: and then he skilfully suggests, that the dignity of Antioch is due not to the greatness of the city, but to S. Peter's having first seated himself there: which honour, great as it was, was nevertheless inferior to that which belongs to the

[g] Mansi, c. 1058.

[h] C. 1045, 1047, &c.

[i] Mansi, c. 1048. He threatened John Bishop of Jerusalem with "exerting the authority of the Apostolic seat, &c." Ibid. c. 1127. See above, p. 24, note [k].

[k] Mansi, c. 1040, 1041.

[l] C. 1051.

place where S. Peter finally settled, viz. his own See, Rome [m].

He claimed absolute authority over the eastern division of Illyria; in which he appointed Rufus, Archbishop of Thessalonica, to be his Vicar and Representative [n]: which is the first instance of the appointment of a Vicar Apostolic. It is supposed [o] that Damasus introduced this office. Innocentius referred to both Damasus and Siricius as authorities for what he did; their letters quoted by him prove that they exercised authority in Illyria; and he says that he was carrying out their intentions [p]. . The circumstances which gave occasion for it are referred to the time of Pope Damasus, when Gratian gave up this province to Theodosius the First,

---

[m] Mansi, c. 1055. [Conf. P. Nicolas I. Mansi, xv. c. 205, &c.]

[n] Mansi, viii. c. 751.

[o] L'Art de Verifier les Dates, vol. iii. in Damasus.

[p] Præcessores nostros Apostolicos imitati, qui beatissimis Acholio et Anysio injungi pro eorum meritis ista voluerunt. In Conc. Rom. A.D. 531. Mansi, viii. c. 751. The letters of Damasus and Siricius referred to were read just before this one of Innocentius. See c. 749.

A. D. 380 [q]; upon which, it is said, Damasus commissioned the Bishop of Thessalonica, Acholius, to act for him, in order that his authority might still be kept up in the province as before [r]. But there is a statute of Theodosius, A. D. 421, which says, that "there shall be no new practices used in Illyria, but the old Canons shall be observed; and if any doubt arise, it shall be determined by a Council, but not without consulting the Archbishop of Constantinople, who enjoys the same prerogative as ancient Rome [s]." This law has been differently interpreted. Some understand it to be a revocation [t] by the Emperor of the authority which the See of Constantinople

[q] Pagi, A.D. 380. vi.

[r] L'Art de Verifier les Dates, as above.

[s] Omni innovatione cessante vetustatem et canones pristinos ecclesiasticos qui nunc usque tenuerunt per omnes Illyrici provincias servari præcipimus. Tum, si quid dubietatis emerserit, id oporteat non absque scientia viri reverendissimi sacrosanctæ legis antistitis urbis Constantinopolitanæ, quæ Romæ veteris prærogativa lætatur, conventui sacerdotali sanctoque judicio reservari. d. prid. id. Jul. Fast. Rom. A. D. 421. c. 4. and Cod, Theod. xvi. Tit. ii. 45. where see Gothofred.

[t] See Pagi, A.D. 421. iv.

had lately acquired over that part of Illyria, and a restoration of the *ancient* authority of the Roman See there. To other readers it would seem that the Emperor prohibited the usurpations of the Roman See over Illyria, and restored to it a Canonical independence. At all events, the reference to the metropolitan authority of Constantinople in doubtful cases, which the law enjoins, directly contradicts the asserted supremacy of Rome.

Pope Innocentius interfered actively at Constantinople in favour of S. Chrysostom, and endeavoured to obtain his restoration : but with no effect, except to exasperate his enemies the more, and to increase the ill feeling now beginning to rise between the Eastern and Western Churches [u].

[u] Sozom. Hist. viii. 26—28. See the Letters which passed, in Mansi, iii. c. 1081—1118. and also in c. 1052, the letter to Maximianus about Atticus. Nicephorus' account of Innocentius' excommunicating all concerned in opposing Chrysostom, including the Emperor Arcadius, and the Emperor's submission printed by Mansi, (which is not given even by Nicephorus,) may well be doubted. Sozomen does not give them. Mansi,

The progress of events in this unhappy discussion, and the correspondence about it which is still extant, throw some light on the history of the Papal power, by shewing the limits within which it was still confined.

Chrysostom's conduct was throughout a protest against the interference of Bishops in foreign Sees; and in writing to the Pope an account of what he had suffered, he refers to the letters of his chief adversary Theophilus, in which even *he* admitted this principle, 'that the Church did not allow causes to be carried into foreign Courts (Ecclesiastical), but they ought to be decided at home in the provincial Synods[v].' This was in strict conformity with the second Canon of the Council of Constantinople, and the sixth of the Council of Nicæa, but directly opposed to the Papal claim of supreme jurisdiction.

---

c. 1118—1125. Nicephor. H. E. xiii. 34, &c. Theodoret does not say this, H. E. v. 34.

[v] Μὴ δεῖν ὑπεροπίους ἕλκεσθαι τὰs δίκαs, ἀλλ' ἐν ταῖs ἐπαρχίαις τὰ τῶν ἐπαρχίων γυμνάζεσθαι. Chrysost. Epist. vol. iii. p. 516.

In his letter S. Chrysostom asked the Pope for sympathy and assistance, but not for his judgment as a superior; neither is there the least hint of any authority belonging to the Pope over the rest of the Church; but, on the contrary, the style and tenor of S. Chrysostom's whole correspondence refutes such an idea.

Moreover, Innocentius himself in reply says, that a General Council was required, because *that alone*ˣ could compose the disturbances of the Church: although a General Council in that age, and long after it, would have been called not by the Pope but by the Emperor. So that even Innocentius did not take to himself authority by virtue of his office to determine all questions in the Church: but he assigned a higher authority to a General Council than he himself possessed; and he claimed much less than some of his successors asserted had always belonged to the Pope by divine right.

Innocentius also witnessed the division of the Empire, and the downfall of the Western half,

---

ˣ Chrysost. Ep. p. 524. Sozomen, H. E. viii. 26.

when Rome was taken and plundered by Alaric.
Some have reckoned this among the causes of
the increase of the Papal power: that the Popes
obtained an ascendancy over the barbarians, who
became rulers instead of subjects.

Socrates attributes to this period the assumption of undue and excessive authority by the
Bishops both of Rome and Alexandria: but he
seems to have applied this chiefly to their strict-
ness in dealing with the Novatians, whose worship
was suppressed in both places[y].

There is extant a fragment of a decree of an
African Council, directing that the quarrel between
the Churches of Rome and Alexandria should be
referred to P. Innocentius, and that they should
abide by his arbitration[z].

In Innocentius' time the great Pelagian controversy broke out. In A. D. 416, a Council at
Carthage, after having condemned Pelagius and
Cælestius, wrote to the Pope, asking him to confirm their humble judgment by the authority of

[y] Socrat. Hist. vii. 7, 9, 11.
[z] Mansi, iii. c. 805.

the Apostolic Chair; (ut statutis nostræ mediocri-
tatis etiam Apostolicæ sedis adhibeatur auctoritas[a].)
Innocentius did not omit to approve of this compliment from the African Fathers, observing how
properly they sought to confirm their own sentence, *as they knew what is due to the Apostolic
seat—for we all who are set in this place desire
to follow the Apostle himself—from whom the very
Episcopate and all the authority of this title proceeded.* (*Scientes quid Apostolicæ sedi debeatur—
cum omnes hoc loco positi ipsum sequi desideremus
Apostolum—a quo ipse Episcopatus et tota auctoritas nominis hujus emersit[b].*) And the Roman
Synod fully concurred in censuring the erroneous
doctrine of Pelagius[c].

But the controversy was carried farther under
P. Zosimus, who succeeded Innocentius, A. D. 417,
and who having been at first persuaded, or en-
trapped, into an approval of Pelagius' doctrines,
had afterwards to retract his judgment, and to

---

[a] Mansi, iv. c. 321.

[b] Mansi, iii. c. 1071.

[c] Ibid. c. 1075.

reconcile this as well as he could with the claim, which he advanced somewhat roundly, and beyond his predecessors apparently, of the infallibility of S. Peter's Chair: which indeed he effected with but a bad grace.

Zosimus ordered that Arles should henceforth be the Metropolitan See of the south of France; Vienne, and the two provinces of Narbonne, being made subject to it[d]. Proculus, the Bishop of Marseilles, resisted this, and, backed by a Synod at Turin[e], ordained some Bishops[f]; but Zosimus would not suffer this to stand: he enjoined all the Bishops here to submit to Arles. The ground on which he founded this Decree was, that *the Church of Arles was founded by Trophimus the Ephesian, sent from Rome for this purpose, who was the first Metropolitan of the province; and that all were in consequence bound to respect this institution of primitive times*[g].

d Ep. v. Mansi, iv. c. 359.

e Spittler remarks, this Synod awarded the claim to Proculus, for his life only. Geschichte des Canonischen Rechts, vol. i. p. 48.

f Ep. vi. vii. c. 361, 363.

g Ep. vii. c. 364, &c. Gregory of Tours names Trophimus, with

It could not be proved in Zosimus' time, that Trophimus ever went to Arles: and even if this were true, it is a most improbable, not to say absurd, supposition, that he was sent on this mission from Rome. This story was the next step after Pope Innocent's declaration about the origin of all the Churches of the West, which was stated just now.

Zosimus went a little beyond all that is preserved of his predecessors in asserting his own authority. He declares in the most explicit terms, that the *Popes inherit from S. Peter a divine authority equal to that of S. Peter*, derived from *the power which our Lord bestowed on him;* so that *no one can question the Pope's decision*[h]. This remarkable statement is made the more extraordinary, by occurring in the same letter in which he retracts his own judgment concerning Cælestius and Pelagius.

The well-known case of Apiarius about this

Dionysius, &c. among the seven Bishops sent into France in the middle of the third century. Hist. Franc. i. 28.

[h] Ep. x. Mansi, iv. c. 366.

time illustrates the history of the Papal Supremacy.

Apiarius[i], a Presbyter of Africa, was degraded
and excommunicated for misconduct by his Bishop, Urbanus of Sicca. He then went to Rome,
and complained to the Pope, who took up his
cause with some warmth; the Pope's interference,
and the claims on which it was founded, were the
subject of discussion in three African Councils at
least.

There was a Canon of the African Church, which
forbad all appeals to foreign Ecclesiastical authorities, under pain of excommunication: but it is
not quite clear when it was made. It might have
been in force before; or it might have grown out
of these proceedings. I cannot trace it farther
back than A. D. 416[k].

Zosimus, as it seems, restored Apiarius, and
alleged, as his authority for doing so, the Canons
of the Council of Nicæa. This was disputed,

---

[i] Epist. Conc. African. Justell. Cod. Can. p. 400.

[k] Conc. Milevit. Can. 22. adopted afterwards in Conc. Carthag.
A. D. 419, &c. Mansi, iv. c. 332. 401.

and the sentence was not received by the Bishop of Sicca. A Council met, in which the Pope's claim was considered; and it was answered, that it did not appear that the Council of Nicæa had decreed thus, according to their copies of the Canons. It was agreed, however, that they would follow the Canons: and in the mean time, until they could verify the authenticity of their own copies, the Roman version of them, as now exhibited, should be allowed. They wrote to this effect to Pope Zosimus[1].

Zosimus sent Legates, a Bishop and two Priests, to Africa; whether they were at the last Council just named, or were sent for the first time to that which presently followed, is not quite clear. But at another Council they appeared: and by their means[m], or persuasion, it seems that Apiarius was on his own petition so

---

[1] Justelli, Cod. Can. p. 402. Quorum omnium de primo et de tertio, &c. priore anno etiam literis nostris, &c. And Mansi, iv. c. 404. Can. 4. De hoc jam superioribus etiam literis concilii nostri rescripsimus.

[m] Justelli, Cod. Can. Eccl. Afr. p. 407.

far restored, that his rank of Priest was allowed
him: but he was forbidden to officiate in the
Church of Sicca [n].

But in this Council, when the Legates were
asked their opinion [o] on the right course of pro-
ceeding with him, they produced a written "Commonitorium," or letter of instructions from Pope
Zosimus, in which they were directed to enquire
specially into four heads of the business before
them, of which, three concerned the question of
appeals, the fourth was, the excommunicating of
the Bishop of Sicca, or summoning him to Rome
for trial, unless he would correct what he had
done wrong: which of course was to be done, if
done, on the ground of maintaining the authority
of Rome against provincial Bishops and Synods,
who would act independently: and it proves, that
the Pope's authority and the Bishop of Sicca,
doubtless with the concurrence of a Synod of
African Bishops, were already at issue.

The Pope's Commonitorium, in which certain

n Justelli, p. 401.　　　o Ibid.

Canons were quoted for those of Nicæa, was considered : but this question did not hinder Apiarius' cause from being so far adjusted, that he was reconciled in the manner above related. An answer was sent to the Pope, but not to Zosimus: Zosimus died Dec. 26, 418 : and the letter of the Council carried back by the Legates was addressed to his successor Bonifacius I, which fixes the date of these proceedings. In the letter, the Council pray that the copies of Canons of Nicæa may be examined at Rome, and that the Pope would write to Alexandria and Constantinople, to request that the Greek copies might be collated there also, in order to learn whether these disputed Canons were really those of Nicæa : but they engaged in the mean time, until this point was settled, to observe the Canons quoted by the Legates [p]. The Council also dispatched a messenger of their own to the Bishops of Antioch, Alexandria, and Constantinople [q], to get copies

[p] Justelli, p. 404.
[q] Mansi, iv. c. 404. (iv.) 407. (ix.)

of the Greek versions of the Canons : and then, as it seems, they adjourned their sittings, in expectation of a fuller meeting on a future day, when they might proceed with the question [r].

When the proposal was made, that a messenger should be sent to examine the copies of the Canons in the Greek Church, and that the Pope should be requested to send also for the same purpose, the Legates proposed (as an amendment) that the Council should request the Pope to examine for himself, and judge what ought to be observed, and that this would be enough [s]; which proposal was not adopted.

The answers to this request, from the Bishops of Alexandria and Constantinople, are dated Nov. 26, 419 [t]. Those Bishops sent authentic copies of the Creed and Canons of Nicæa, with a letter of certification of each. When they arrived in Africa, the Council sent them on to the Pope [u].

---

[r] Mansi, c. 402. (i.)

[s] Mansi, c. 405. (v.)

[t] Justelli, p. 404, 406.   The letter is also in Mansi, iv. c. 515.

[u] Justelli, p. 409.

What more was done during the life of Bonifacius does not appear : he died A. D. 422, and
was succeeded by Cælestinus; under whom the
question was renewed. For Apiarius presented
himself before him also, appealed to his authority,
was received with favour, and actually restored [x].
Cælestinus then sent the same Legates again, who
had before gone into Africa : a Council was called
to meet them, by whom the question was heard.
There seem now to have been some new charges
of misconduct made against Apiarius : certainly
one distinct complaint against him was his con-
tumacy in resisting the authority of his own
Church, in the African Synods : and in the enquiry now made, which employed the Council
for three days, the Legates are said to have tried
what they could to delay the proceedings against
him.   At last, however, he unexpectedly made a
confession of his guilt, which is represented to
have been gross irregularities, though not speci-
fied; and so the Council concluded with a letter
to the Pope.

x Justelli, p. 407.

In this ʸ, after giving a short account of what had been done, they request that the Pope will not in future receive persons excommunicated by their Synods, which they observe is contrary to the Canons of Nicæa; they protest against appeals to foreign tribunals; they deny the Pope's right to send Legates to exercise jurisdiction in his name, which they say is not authorized by any Canon of the Fathers, and that the ˌpretended Nicene Canons alleged in support of it were not in any of the authentic copies of the Canons of Nicæa; they request that the Pope will not send any agents, or Nuncios, to interfere with them in any business, *for fear the Church should suffer through pride and ambition;* and they hint, that Africa has had quite as much of the late Legate Faustinus as it can bear.

Such was the judgment of the African Church on the question of the Papal Supremacy.

The Canons quoted by the Legates, under the

ʸ See the Letter in Justelli, p. 408, and Mansi as quoted above.

title of Nicæa, were in fact those of Sardica[z], which Council was not received by the Greek nor the African Church. How Zosimus, Bonifacius, and Cælestinus, (for the last two sent the same Legates, and never retracted what Zosimus had instructed them to advance,) came to quote them falsely, is the question. But it is to be observed, that the same thing had been done apparently by others before them. Innocentius I. in the Decrees which he sent to the Church of Rouen, in one of his Epistles, seems to refer to the Council of Nicæa for the Canons in support of the appellate jurisdiction of Rome[a].

The Romanists are at some pains to shew, that the Canons of Sardica are a kind of outwork to the Council of Nicæa[b], designed merely to carry out and secure the same principles, and

---

[z] The apparent acknowledgment of this in one part (only) in Mansi, c. 405. (vi.) is probably an interpolation, as Binius judged. See his note, c. 418. l.

[a] Can. 3. Mansi, iii. c. 1033. Quesnel ad Ep. Leon. v. 4. p. 430.

[b] See the account of the Council of Sardica, and notes, &c. in Mansi.

therefore that both are really one and the same thing, and Sardica might be quoted as a part of Nicæa, or virtually contained in it; a mode of construing the authority of a written document, which could not be much more admitted by lawyers on the point of law, than it would be by moralists on the question of right.

It has been also said [c] in explanation, that it was the practice in the Books of Canons to subjoin the Canons of Sardica after those of Nicæa, so that the title of Nicæa would stand at the head of both; and either might be quoted under that name. But it is not probable that the Popes should have been so ignorant as to quote thus inadvertently: and if so done designedly, it does not much help towards their justification. I fear we must say, that we are come now to the age of *papal forgeries*, whether the acts of Popes themselves, or of the officials of their Courts.

---

[c] Spittler suggests this, to account for Maruthas' attributing seventy-three Canons to the Council of Nicæa. See Assemani, Bibl. Or. i. p. 193. Spittler, Geschichte des Canonisch. Rechts, p. 99.

And the imposition, although once detected and exposed, did not cease : for Pope Leo, little more than twenty-five years afterwards, A. D. 449, again alleged the authority of the Council of Nicæa for the Sardican Canons, concerning the right of appeal [d]. And Zonaras speaks of it as the practice of Rome [e], "the Bishops of Rome falsely say, that this is the Canon of the first General Council of Nicæa."

There is preserved a copy of a Roman [f] Book of Canons, which is supposed to be as old as this age, and to have been in use in Pope Innocentius' I. time; which is referred to [g] for a specimen of the manner in which other Canons were added, under the title of the Council of Nicæa. Here forty-six are given; whereas only twenty were made at Nicæa, and only twenty-one at

[d] Leon. Ep. xl. where see Quesnel; and also on Ep. v. 4. p. 430. Comp. below, p. 60.

[e] Ad Can. 5. Conc. Sardic. Bevereg. Synod. p. 489.

[f] Codex Canonum et Constitutorum Ecclesiæ Romanæ, Append. ad Leonis Opera, Quesnelli.

[g] By Gieseler, Kirchl. Geschichte.

Sardica; so that even more than the Sardican arc here described as those of Nicæa.

But I observe another peculiarity: in the Canon of Sardica, (among these forty-six given as of Nicæa) which authorized Bishops to appeal to Rome, the name of the then Pope Julius appears in the original of the Council of Sardica, A. D. 347: but in this Roman book, instead of Julius there appears the name of *Silvester* [h], who was the Pope at the time of the Council of Nicæa. If therefore that Codex Canonum et Constitutorum with this reading was really in use in Pope Innocentius' time, it proves a deliberate fraud to have been practised, even in that age, by some one who wished to make this Canon of Sardica, made under Pope Julius, pass for a Canon made at Nicæa in the time of Pope Silvester.

It was by means of such collections as this

---

[h] Can. 30. Mansi says the same thing appears in some copies of the Canons of Sardica in Dionysius Exiguus, *Quidam MSS. habent Sylvestro.* Can. 3. Conc. Sard. Mans. iii. c. 23. See also an account of spurious Canons, which passed in the East, under the title of Nicæa, in Renaudot, Hist. Patriarch. Alexandr. xix. p. 71. Par. 1713.

"Canons and Constitutions," that in course of time the Decretals grew up, afterwards so notorious among the corruptions of the Roman Church. So suspicious a beginning, as this which has been described, might lead on without much difficulty to a system of falsification, which certainly was active at some time. There are forged epistles or decrees attributed to many Popes [i], from the days of S. Peter downwards. Under the names of Julius and Damasus, especially, as well as Innocentius I, there are some writings, which, if genuine, would be taken for explicit testimony in favour of the theory of the Papal Supremacy, of which they speak in language at variance with the authentic documents of that age. But it cannot be determined at what time these forgeries were composed.

One incident belonging to this period, although not connected with the dispute in the African Church, ought not to be omitted.

Pope Bonifacius I, who succeeded Zosimus, was

---

[i] See Mansi, under the "*Vita*" and "*Epistolæ*" of each Pope.

opposed by a rival, who was elected Anti-pope
by his own party, and consecrated by three who
were or passed for Bishops. The Clergy who
had elected Bonifacius, on this appealed[k] to the
Emperor Honorius, and prayed that the Anti-
pope Eulalius might be summoned and tried by
the Emperor's Court; where they engaged that
they would appear with Pope Bonifacius, and
declare who was truly elected. The Pope himself also petitioned[l] the Emperor not to allow
such disorderly acts, as had been lately committed: and the Emperor, in answer[m], published
an edict, that in future, if ever two rival Popes
were elected, neither should be Pope, but a new
election should be made.

[k] Mansi, iv. c. 390.   [l] Ibid. c. 391.   [m] Ibid. c. 393.

LECTURE II.

POPE CÆLESTINUS, under whom the question raised by Apiarius came to an end, was much concerned in the Pelagian controversy: two important letters of his are extant, in which he gave his own judgment on some of the disputed points, against both the Pelagians and the Semi-pelagians, asserted the authority of S. Augustine's works, and endeavoured to restrain the further progress of the controversy[a].

We find also from other letters, that he exercised authority in the South of France, as well as in Italy[b].

In the proceedings of the Council of Ephesus, A.D. 431, he took a conspicuous part. He de-

[a] Mansi, iv. c. 454, 458, &c.
[b] Mansi, c. 464, 469.

puted Cyril of Alexandria to act as his representative, and with his authority. To Nestorius, then
Patriarch of Constantinople, he sent a command,
"that he should retract his disputed opinions,
and conform to the faith of Rome, Alexandria,
and the Catholic Church, within ten days, under
penalty of being *ipso facto* excommunicated."
He wrote also to the Clergy of Constantinople;
to the Bishop of Antioch; to the Council; to the
Emperor Theodosius; to Cyril of Alexandria
again; and the Council wrote to him.

No notice of S. Peter and the divine right of
Supremacy appears in any of these, nor in that
which he wrote to Maximinian, the successor of
Nestorius. But in one written to the Council
after Nestorius was condemned, and also one to
the Clergy and people of Constantinople, he speaks
of S. Peter's care over the whole Church[c].

The result of this great contest in the Church
must have been favourable to the influence of
Rome: for Rome on this, as on other occasions,
was the champion of orthodoxy, which ultimately

[c] Mansi, v. c. 268, 275.

prevailed: while the divisions, which arose on other grounds than doctrine alone, between the Oriental and the Egyptian Bishops, by weakening the union of the Eastern Church, gave fresh authority to the Primate of the West; and the name of S. Peter, as the guarantee for the apostolic faith, could the more easily claim the deference of an assumed supremacy. " You[d] have proved, by the event of this business, what it is to agree with us. Saint Peter the Apostle has delivered by his successors. that which he received. Who would wish to *separate from the teaching of him, whom the Master Himself taught, as the chief among the Apostles ?* " said the next Pope, Sixtus, writing in triumph to the Bishop of Antioch after the reconciliation.

Pope Sixtus, or Sextus, III. who succeeded Cælestine, A. D. 432, was accused of some mis-

---

[d] "Expertus es negotii præsentis eventu, quid sit sentire nobiscum. Beatus Petrus Apostolus in successoribus suis quod accepit hoc tradidit. Quis ab ejus se velit separare doctrina, quem ipse inter Apostolos primum Magister edocuit?" Mansi, c. 379. As if S. Peter's teaching had been different from that of S. Paul, or S. James, or S. John !

conduct by a certain Bassus: on which the Emperor Valentinian III. ordered him to summon
a Council. He did so; and when the case was
examined, the Pope was completely cleared, and
his accuser Bassus was condemned, excommunicated, and his property confiscated, which the
Emperor gave to the Church. Bassus died very
soon afterwards[e]. The Pope, writing an account
of this to the Oriental Bishops, takes some pains
to shew, that his trial by the Council was his
own free act, that he was under no obligation[f]
to submit to it if he had not wished it, and
that it established no precedent for any of his
successors.

This assertion, coupled with the fact, that the
Patriarch of Constantinople had been tried by the
Council of Ephesus just before, and condemned
for heresy, amounts to *a claim of exemption from
all ecclesiastical jurisdiction,* unless he meant to
draw a distinction between a Roman and a General

[e] Mansi, v. c. 1155, 1156.

[f] He quotes the Law to prove this; viz. that the indictment
ought to have been made in writing, &c. c. 1155.

Council. But perhaps the fact, that he was tried, may be as good evidence one way, as his assertion would be the others.

Pope Leo, who succeeded Sixtus III, A. D. 440, did much to advance the authority of the See.

In spite of the opposition which Pope Cælestinus had found in Africa, he, soon after he entered his office, sent a Legate there to inquire into some irregular practices in the ordination of Bishops and Priests, which he had heard reported by persons who came from that country[h].

In Illyria, following the steps of Innocentius I. and his predecessors[i], he appointed Anastasius, Bishop of Thessalonica, his Vicar Apostolic, asserting his right to do this, because *our Lord gave the primacy of the Apostles to S. Peter as a reward for his faith,* and therefore *he (Leo) was bound to take care of all Churches.* He authorized his Vicar to be his representative in all

[g] Was it the wish to shew this claim the stronger, which made some later hand compose the account of the pretended trial of Polychronius, Bishop of Jerusalem, at Rome, &c. ? Mansi, c. 1170.

[h] Leon. Ep. i. p. 203. Ed. Quesnel. fol. 1700. [i] Ep. xii. 1.

cases[k]; to consecrate the Metropolitan Bishops,
who also were not to consecrate their Suffragans
without consulting the Vicar; to call Councils
twice a year, requiring the Bishops (two named
by each Metropolitan from his own province) to
attend; to determine all cases; or if necessary,
and in cases of appeal, to send them to Rome[l];
which he affirmed to be " according[m] to the
Canons," referring apparently to *those of Sardica*,
again.

To this Decree the Metropolitans of Achaia
wrote in answer, signifying their consent[n].

___

k Ep. v. 2. Comp. also Ep. xii. 11, where he asserts S. Peter's
power among the Apostles, among whom, though equal all in
" *dignity*" and " *election*," &c. there was a " *difference in power*,"
which he takes for the origin of the difference of power among
Bishops, viz. Metropolitans and others. The Pope, as S. Peter's
successor, being supreme over all. This fancy was adopted and
improved upon in later ages, when the Supremacy was more
" developed ;" and then it was said, " *S. Peter governed the Church
with the assistance of the Apostles, as the Pope does with the assistance of the Cardinals.*" Kalteisen, Orat. in Canis. Thesaur. iv.
p. 650.

l See all these and other things defined in Ep. v. and Ep. xii.

m Ep. v. 5, where see Quesnel's note 4. p. 430.

n Ep. xiii.

Leo was engaged (A. D. 445) in an important cause concerning the South of France.

Pope Zosimus had decreed[o] that Arles should be the Metropolitan See of this province, and that all the Churches of Vienne and the two provinces of Narbonne should be subject to the Archbishop of Arles, and[p] he forbad Hilary Bishop of Narbonne (2da) from all Metropolitan rights. This he did, as was said before, (p. 39) on the ground, that Trophimus had first founded the Church of Arles, being sent thither by S. Peter from Rome, and that such had always been the privileges of the Church of Arles. Patroclus the Bishop of Arles, on the strength of this, had two years afterwards filled up a vacant Bishopric in the province of Narbonne; on which complaint was made to the then Pope Bonifacius; who, in a letter to Hilary Bishop of Narbonne, condemned it as contrary to the Canons of Nicæa against encroaching on the rights of episcopal provinces, and authorized the Bishop of Narbonne to take cognizance of the case as Metropolitan, and to

---

[o] Mansi, iv. c. 359. A.D. 417.   [p] Ibid. c. 363, 364, 365.

correct the wrong done; and desired him then to send a report to Rome [q].

Pope Cælestinus also, nine years afterwards, had prohibited all encroachment of one Metropolitan on another, in a letter to the Bishops of Vienne and Narbonne, referring to Pope Bonifacius' letter as a precedent[r].

In Pope Leo's time, another Hilary, Bishop of Arles, claimed Metropolitan authority over Vienne: he ordained some Bishops there: deposed one, Celidonius[s], and superseded another who was sick, Projectus, by ordaining one in his place; and spoke lightly of the authority of S. Peter and the Pope's Supremacy[t]. For this reason, Leo, in a Synod at Rome, where both Hilary and Celidonius were heard, decreed, that

[q] Mansi, c. 395. A.D. 419.   [r] Ibid. c. 466. A.D. 428.

[s] Celidonius has been often called Bishop of Vesontium (Besançon): but Quesnel argues at length to shew that he was Bishop of Vienne. See Dissert. v. in Leon. Opp. v. ii. p. 228. where this question is discussed, and Hilarius defended. Quesnel in conclusion condemns Pope Leo for encroaching on the rights of the Gallican Church in particular, and violating the order of the Church in general, in his conduct in the case.

[t] Leon. Ep. x. 2, &c.

Hilary should lose all his Metropolitan rights, which should be transferred to Vienne; he nominated another Bishop (Leontius), to whom he gave the power of calling Synods in the place of Hilary: and the deposed Bishop Celidonius was restored[u]. This was followed up by a law of the Emperor Valentinian III. confirming the Pope's sentence: in which the Pope's Supremacy is fully acknowledged; and it is said that his sentence would have had authority without this law[x]. The date of this was A. D. 445. The concluding sentence of the law is remarkable. "We[y] decree, by a perpetual sanction, that nothing shall be attempted against ancient custom by the Bishops of Gaul, or other provinces, without the

---

[u] Leon. Ep. x.   [x] Ibid. Ep. post x.

[y] Perenni sanctione decernimus, ne quid tam episcopis Gallicanis, quam aliarum provinciarum, contra consuetudinem veterem liceat sine venerabilis papæ urbis æternæ auctoritate temptare. Sed illis, omnibusque pro lege sit, quidquid sanxit, vel sanxerit apostolicæ sedis auctoritas, ita ut quisquis episcoporum ad judicium Romani antistitis evocatus venire neglexerit, per moderatorem ejusdem provinciæ adesse cogatur. Novell. Theodos. Codex Theod. Tit. xxiv. Supplement. p. 67. Gothofred. ed. Lips. 1741.

authority of the venerable Pope of the eternal city : but whatever the authority 'of the Apostolic Chair ordains, shall be law to them; so that if any Bishop when summoned shall omit to come to the court of the Roman Bishop, he shall be compelled to come by the governor of the province."

Thus the Pope's Supremacy (to a certain extent in appellate jurisdiction) was now established, not by the law of Christ, nor by a Canon of the Church over the Church, but by the Roman law over the dominions of the Roman emperor of the West.

The Pope in this cause could hardly avoid noticing the former papal sentence in favour of the Church of Arles. He did this very shortly; saying it was "a favour first granted to Patroclus by the Apostolic Chair for a time only, which upon reconsideration was afterwards withdrawn[z]:" which plainly contradicts the reason assigned for it by Pope Zosimus himself, namely, Apostolic institution and primitive custom, which

---

[z] Id quod nullus decessorum ipsius ante Patroclum habuit—quod Patroclo a sede apostolica temporaliter videbatur esse concessum, postmodum sit sententia meliore sublatum, &c. Ep. x. 4.

he puts forward as if they established an un-
alienable right.

After Bishop Hilary's death, when Ravennius
had been ordained to succeed him, the Bishop
and Clergy of the province petitioned [a] the Pope,
A.D. 450, to restore to Arles the ancient Metropolitan dignity, which it had inherited from
Trophimus. They made much use of Trophimus'
name in their letter: indeed it is more likely
that this legend, which Pope Zosimus had dwelt
upon before, was coined at Arles than at Rome.
The Bishop of Vienne had already complained of
the (new) Bishop of Arles. Leo took the settlement of the question into his hands, and decreed
a kind of compromise. He received favourably
the petitioner's request [b], "that what the last
Bishop had deservedly lost by his presumption
might now be restored;" and finding, as he said,
that both the Churches of Arles, and of Vienne,

[a] Leon. Ep. post xlix.

[b] Leon. Ep. l. 1, &c. He could not but approve of their letter;
for their argument is, "Arles has the supremacy of Gaul, because
Trophimus received it by commission from S. Peter, and it has
been confirmed by Popes."

F

were ancient and honourable, he awarded to the Bishop of Vienne, Vienne and four neighbouring cities, and gave the rest of the province to Arles[c].

Thus Rome grew now by means of whatever was faulty in the Church, as before she had grown by her own merits. Pride and love of power among the provincial Churches forged a yoke for themselves, which the ambition of the Popes was not slow to lay on their necks; and time, with each succeeding disorder, political or religious, riveted it more firmly.

You remember how prominent the name of Pope Leo was in the second Council of Ephesus, the "*Latrocinium,*" A.D. 449. The omitting to read his Epistle in that Council was one of the offences for which Dioscorus, Patriarch of Alexandria, was afterwards condemned.

Leo had before this corresponded with Dioscorus. There is a letter extant in which he asserts his supremacy over Alexandria, by sug-

[c] [In a letter on this subject is a remarkable assertion, that grace is received by the Church through S. Peter, &c. beginning with, Sed hujus muneris sacramentum, &c. Leon. Ep. x. 1, which was quoted by the Patriarch of Antioch at Constance. L'Enf. Hist. du Conc. i. p. 191. ed. Amst. 1727.]

gesting that, since *our Lord bestowed the Su-premacy on Peter*, and *Rome followed S. Peter*, it would be "*shameful* [d]" *if his pupil S. Mark should hold anything different at Alexandria.*

After the Council (2d of Ephesus) was over, and the outrages committed there had been reported at Rome, Leo addressed the Emperor Theodosius, praying him to call a General Council in Italy to rectify the irregularities of the late Council at Ephesus: in which letter, in vague and somewhat obscure terms, he seems to assert a power derived from S. Peter to exercise some control over Councils, and implies that the calling a General Council, such as he asked for, would be the referring of the question to Rome as the Supreme Court of Appeal, according to the Canons of Nicæa; that is to say, *again, Sardica* [e].

Those who had suffered from Dioscorus' violence at the Council of Ephesus, A. D. 449, looked to Rome, as usual, for protection. Flavianus before his death had appealed to Rome [f] appa-

---

[d] *Nefas.* Leon. Ep. xi.

[e] Leon. Ep. xxxix. and the same again in Synod. Ep. xl.

[f] Liberat. Brev. 12. Leon. Ep. xxxix. It is possible, however, that he appealed to a General Council.

rently. Theodoret wrote to the Pope, and referred his cause to the Pope's judgment, with an urgent request for his assistance. His letter is full of expressions of deference and respect for the Pope, both personally, and in regard to his See: but it is remarkable, that he allows him precedence, and every honour, except that Supremacy derived by divine right from S. Peter, which the Popes now were so fond of asserting or insinuating in their own writings g: which indeed never appears in any communication from the Greek Bishops, though now so commonly acknowledged in the Western Church.

When Anatolius was elected Patriarch of Constantinople in the place of Flavianus, who had lost his life in the second Council of Ephesus, Leo, not without reason, hesitated a little before receiving him into Communion; until he had ascertained that he was clear from the errors of Nestorius or Eutyches, and from all share in the outrages done to Flavianus h.

g Leon. Ep. post xlvii. and Theodoret, Ep. cxiii.
h Leon. Ep. liii. liv. lix. lx. &c.

Leo much opposed the calling of the Council of Chalcedon. He first asked for one to be called in Italy: and then that the meeting proposed for Nicæa first, and afterwards Chalcedon, might be deferred. He also [i] asked, that no discussion might be allowed concerning the faith.

When the Council met, he sent his Legates to attend, who took precedence of all the other Bishops: and when judgment was finally given on Dioscorus, the Legates pronounced it in the Pope's name, as if it was his sentence. Whether this was at all the reason why the Council made the Canon which so much offended him, does not appear. But that Canon, made in spite of his Legates, which *gave to the See of Constantinople a dignity equal in rank and next in place to Rome* [j], drew forth all the opposition which he could make.

[i] Ep. lxxiv.

[j] The Canon is the 28th of the Counc. Chalced. as follows: "Following always the decrees of the holy Fathers, and acknowledging the Canon which has just been read of the 150 pious Bishops who met in Council in New Rome, the royal city of Constantinople, (the second General Council, A. D. 381)

The Synodical letter of the Council to him is written in a friendly and respectful tone, complimentary both to him and to his See; but of course it speaks with entire independence of those things which had been decreed; to which it asks for his concurrence.

in the reign of the late king Theodosius the Great of pious memory, we also decree and resolve the same concerning the precedence of the holy Church of the same New Rome (or) Constantinople. For the Fathers with reason gave precedence to the Chair of Old Rome, because that was the royal city. And with the same object in view, the 150 pious Bishops gave equal precedence to the holy Chair of New Rome ; rightly judging, that the city which is honoured by the royal residence and the Senate, and enjoys equal precedence with the elder royal city of Rome, should also have rank like her in ecclesiastical respects also, being next after her. So that the Metropolitan Bishops of Pontus, Asia, and Thrace, only, and also the Bishops among the barbarians of these same provinces, shall be ordained by the aforesaid holy Chair (Bishop) of the holy Church at Constantinople. Provided that each Metropolitan of the aforesaid provinces, together with the Bishops of the province, shall ordain the Bishops of the province, as directed by the holy Canons. And that the Metropolitan of the aforesaid provinces shall be ordained, as aforesaid, by the Archbishop of Constantinople, the votes agreeing, according to custom, and being given for him." From the Greek Text in Routh, Opuscula, ii. p. 68.

The Emperor Marcian wrote to the same effect: the Pope answered it with loud complaints of the ambition of Anatolius; he wrote also to the Empress Pulcheria; and exhorted both to use their authority to restrain Anatolius, to whom he addressed another letter of remonstrance, ending with a hint of the possibility of excommunication, if he persisted in his " unlawful" course [k]. To the Empress he writes [l], that *by S. Peter's authority he absolutely annuls the Decree of Chalcedon.*

The Pope's argument in all this was, that the Decree of Chalcedon concerning Constantinople was contrary to the Canons of Nicæa: and that no Council could ever change what had been decreed at Nicæa.

We have already seen, that he called the Canons made at Sardica the Canons of Nicæa: so that of course he would have comprehended all these Canons in this assertion of an immutable (or divine) authority. Which assertion, we must

[k] Ep. lxxx. 6.
[l] Ep. lxxix. 3.   See Quesnel, note.

observe, was in direct contradiction to the judgment of the Council of Nicæa itself[m]: for in that
Council it was decided, that the judgment of one
Council might be reviewed by another Council
(not by the Pope). At the same time he also
expressly rejected the authority of the Council of
Constantinople, A. D. 381 [n].

He also objected that Constantinople was not
an Apostolic See, and therefore ought not to have
precedence before Alexandria and Antioch: I do
not find that he urged anything in behalf of the
dignity of the still more ancient Apostolic See,
Jerusalem [o].

And in the course of the argument he pleads,
that the ambition of Constantinople, in thus
assuming power over Alexandria and Antioch,

---

[m] Athanas. Apol. c. Ar. 22. p. 142.

[n] Ep. lxxx. 5, where see Quesnel's note, and Ep. lxxix. 2.
Pope Vigilius uses the same kind of language in his *" Constitu-
tum,"* *in favour* of the Council of Chalcedon : but with a pointed
and remarkable reservation, that is, in all those matters which
were transacted with the co-operation of the Legates of Rome, &c.
Mansi, ix. c. 103, &c.

[o] Juvenal is named in Ep. xcii. 4.

encroached on the rights of all the Metropolitans[p] in those countries, in language which an impartial reader might think to be a stronger argument, and a severer reproof, against Rome than against Constantinople.

It is curious too to observe, in his defence of the independence of Alexandria and Antioch, how adroitly he connects them both with Rome, and presses both into the service of his theory of S. Peter's Supremacy[q]. Alexandria was the Church of S. Peter's companion and disciple S. Mark, and therefore was to be tenderly regarded for S. Peter's sake; and Antioch was the Church of S. Peter's own foundation, where he first presided with special authority until he transferred his seat to Rome. Which line of argument, while it plausibly upheld the rank of those two Churches against Constantinople, effectually excluded them from competing with the supremacy of Rome.

There was another point also determined at

---

[p] Ep. lxxx. 2.
[q] Ep. lxxx. 5. xcii. 2.

Chalcedon which could hardly have pleased Pope Leo, although it is not distinctly noticed by him as an objection.

The Council informed him of two things; the decree that Constantinople should exercise Metropolitical authority over Asia, Pontus, and Thrace; and that which gave Constantinople rank immediately after Rome; and to these he strongly objected.

But besides these, the ninth of the Canons[r] related to the question of Appeals; in which it decreed, that Clergy should appeal from their own Bishop to the provincial Synod : but Bishops or Clergy should appeal from their Metropolitan to the Exarch of the province, (Patriarch) or else to the Bishop of Constantinople : with no mention of Rome. Therefore this Canon was directly opposed to the supreme appellate jurisdiction which Rome had claimed on the strength of the Canons of Sardica.

It appears then, that the authority which the See of Rome pretended to possess, even in the

---

[r] Routh, Opuscula, ii. p. 58, &c.

fifth century, was *in open contradiction to the Canons of two General Councils,* viz. (the second) of Constantinople, and (the fourth) of Chalcedon. But Rome advanced much farther in her pretensions afterwards.

This dispute produced a coolness between Rome and Constantinople, but not an absolute breach. They still corresponded: the Pope sometimes still offering advice, and interfering in the government of the Church, in a way which did not please the Patriarch*: but they continued to write to each other, although with some intervals of silence, as friends.

The Pope complained, that one of his own friends, Julian, Bishop of Cos, to whom he had given a commission to act with his Legates*, favoured the views of Anatolius*, and did not respond, as formerly, to his own zeal in behalf of the Eastern Church. He wished Julian to be his agent in collecting and sending

* Ep. cxxviii.
t Ep. lxvi. lxxi. lxxxix. 2.
u Ep. lxxxi.

information of everything that concerned the faith at Constantinople[x]. Perhaps Julian did not concur in the absolute authority which the Pope claimed over the East as well as the West.

Another complaint of the Pope was[y], that Anatolius required the Illyrian Bishops to *subscribe to him*, that is, profess canonical obedience. Although, as we have seen, Leo, like some of his predecessors, had claimed entire command of the Illyrian Church, and appointed the Archbishop of Thessalonica his Vicar Apostolic.

A. D. 455, Rome was taken and plundered by the Vandals under Genseric. A. D. 457, Leo succeeded Marcian on the Imperial throne. And a little before his accession came that outrage in Alexandria, when Proterius the Patriarch was murdered by the party who opposed the Council of Chalcedon, and Timothy Ælurus was elected in his place. This caused a great revolution in the Church of Egypt; the supporters of the Council of Chalcedon were driven out: many

[x] Ep. xcviii.
[y] Ep. lxxxviii. 5.

Bishops took refuge at Constantinople: and the dominant party endeavoured to get the Emperor to call another General Council, intending to reverse what was done at Chalcedon.

Pope Leo used his influence on this occasion with good success. He addressed letters to Constantinople, and to Bishops elsewhere; and especially to the Emperor Leo, urging him strongly to maintain both the orthodox faith, and the cause of ecclesiastical order, and not to allow questions to be reopened, which had been already fully determined[z]. He also, by the Emperor's desire, sent Legates to Constantinople[a].

It is probable, that the Emperor's measures for restoring peace, and ejecting the turbulent party at Alexandria, were due in part to the energy of Pope Leo.

The Pope lived to see the intruder Timothy Ælurus driven from Alexandria, the authority of the Council of Chalcedon acknowledged, and

[z] Ep. cxv. &c. to cxxxiv.
[a] Ep. cxxxiii.

his rival Anatolius succeeded by Gennadius in
the See of Constantinople; and died A. D. 461,
having done good service to the Church in
defending the truth by his courage and ability,
actuated doubtless by high motives and dis-
interested zeal, but having also contributed in
no small degree to lay the foundation of that
fabric of secular power in the assumed Supremacy, which afterwards became so fatal to the
Roman Church.

Under the next two Popes, Hilary (Hilarus)
A. D. 461, and Simplicius, A. D. 468, there was
not much that throws any new light on the
question of the Papal authority.

Under Hilarus, the dispute about the limits of
their jurisdiction was revived between the Bishops
of Arles and of Narbonne, and, as before, referred
to the Pope, who gave judgment upon it, by inhibiting the Bishop of Narbonne from exercising
Metropolitan authority [b].

In a Synod at Rome, A. D. 465, a Canon

---

[b] Mansi, vii. c. 934.

appears, ordering that the *Pope's Decrees* (*Apostolicæ sedis decreta*) should be observed inviolate by the Clergy, together with the Divine Constitutions, under pain of deposition [c].

Pope Simplicius (A. D. 468) is said to have instituted the custom, that the Priests should take weekly turns of hearing confessions of penitents, and baptizing in the three principal Churches at Rome [d]. The Priest, whose turn it was to officiate for the week, was called Hebdomadarius [e].

In his correspondence with some of the Bishops whose conduct was censured, Simplicius uses a tone of authority. He requires the Archbishop of Ravenna to make over a certain piece of land to another person for life; and threatens him with the loss of his Metropolitan privileges [f]: another he mulcts of three fourths of his revenue, and requires him to refund what he has received more than this [g].

---

[c] Mansi, c. 960.
[d] Ibid. c. 970, &c.
[e] Binius, note in c. 971.
[f] Ibid. c. 972.
[g] Ibid. c. 973.

In Simplicius' time, (or, as some say [h], at the
end of his life, while the See was vacant) two
laws were made concerning the Popedom by
Odoacer, then King in Italy. The first was,
that, to prevent disturbances in the State, no
Pope should be elected without consent of the
King. This Odoacer said he did by the advice
of Pope Simplicius. The other was, that no
future Pope should alienate any property, land,
chattels, or anything else which belonged, or
ever should belong, to the Church. These laws
would have been important. But they were both
annulled, i. e. declared to be invalid, in a Synod
at Rome under Pope Symmachus, A. D. 502. It
was argued, that they had no subscription from
the Pope, nor ecclesiastical authority, to back
them; and that laymen could not interfere to
legislate on these subjects [i].

During Simplicius' lifetime there were great
disputes about the See of Alexandria, which had

---

[h] Baronius, ad an. 483.
[i] Mansi, viii. c. 266.

been seized by Timothy Ælurus. Simplicius wrote to Constantinople on this subject, and on the question of the Council of Chalcedon, and the controversy arising out of it. I observe, that, in his letters to the Emperor Zeno, he plainly asserts the Roman Supremacy, and scarcely in any letter fails to introduce some reference to S. Peter[k]; but in his letters to Acacius and the Clergy of Constantinople, he never alludes to that subject, except it be once in the title, *Sedes Apostolica*, to the Clergy.

Acacius, the then Patriarch of Constantinople, had always adhered to the Council of Chalcedon, and opposed those who rejected it; but when, after that party had elected Peter Mongus to the See of Alexandria, and he had been ejected by the orthodox[l], the Pope urged Acacius to press the Emperor to banish Peter and his followers from the empire, Acacius did not attend to his request; although the Pope himself also asked

---

[k] Mansi, c. vii. 975, 981, 984, 988.

[l] Epist. Acacii, Mansi, c. 982. This was between 476 and 489, when Timothy Salophaciolus died. Liberat. 16.

the Emperor to do this [m]. A few years afterwards, on the death of the orthodox Bishop Timothy Salophaciolus, Peter Mongus was allowed by the Emperor to retain the See of Alexandria, on condition of his receiving the doctrinal edict called the *Henoticon* [n]. Whether the foresight of this had conduced to deter Acacius from joining in the Pope's application against Peter Mongus, or whether he thought that it was on other grounds unnecessary, does not appear.

Acacius had also (at the Emperor's desire) ordained a Bishop of Antioch, by virtue of his Metropolitan authority, according to the Canon of Chalcedon. The Pope was not pleased at this, upon the old ground on which so great objection had been raised against the rank given to Constantinople. He would not say anything against what had been then done for Antioch with the Emperor's concurrence; but he prayed that this might be no precedent for the future, since it was, he said, against the Canons of Nicæa.

[m] Ep. Simpl. Mansi, vii. c. 986.
[n] Evagr. iii. 13.

And the Pope rather complained that Acacius had not assented to his request about Peter Mongus, and had been backward of late in his correspondence with him, although he was confident of the soundness of Acacius' faith [o]. When Peter Mongus was confirmed by the Emperor at Alexandria, his opponent John was supported by the Pope [p].

Thus a coolness arose [q] between Rome and Constantinople for about the last [r] three years of Simplicius' life.

When P. Felix II. succeeded, A. D. 483, the question soon came to an issue.

Felix took up the cause of the competitor of Peter Mongus for the See of Alexandria, one

---

[o] Mansi, vii. c. 987, 988.

[p] Ibid. c. 992. Comp. Evagr. iii. 12.

[q] Mansi, vii. c. 991, 992, 995.

[r] Cum fere per triennium ne in id veniret, apostolicæ sedis epistolis doceatur competenter instructus. Epist. Gelas. Mansi, viii. c. 33. The editor reckons this A. D. 478—480, saying, " alium init calculum Liberatus." Comp. Gelasius again, per triennium fere litteris destinatis eundem monere non destitit. Mansi, viii. c. 52 and 65.

John, whom the Emperor had banished on a charge of breaking his oath, and who had fled to Rome for protection. He complained that Peter Mongus was unlawfully ordained to the See, and that he was a heretic; and he charged Acacius not to hold communion with him, and to urge the Emperor to take measures against him and his party [s].

When these remonstrances had been made for some time without effect, he sent Legates to Constantinople, with a commission to try and depose Peter Mongus. The Legates were not received: but were even arrested, and treated with some roughness; and after some time, they were actually prevailed on to hold communion, in reality or in appearance, with Peter Mongus and his party. When the Pope heard of this, he recalled them, and in Synod at Rome deposed them; they were Bishops.

The letter which he sent by them to Acacius at first was not conciliatory: he lectured Acacius roundly for his remissness, and falling away from

[s] Liberat. 18.

his former zeal in defending the faith against all heretical devices : and he did not forget to notice among his misdemeanours, his presumption in setting himself up against the reverence due to S. Peter : indeed he here uses no reserve, but claims *absolute and perpetual authority for* the *censura*[t] *beatissimi Petri,* i. e. the judgment of the Pope. He wrote also a pressing letter against Peter Mongus to the Emperor, appealing to him in the name of S. Peter[u].

He exercised his authority also towards the Church of Antioch, by sending a sentence of deposition and anathema[x] on Peter the Fuller, who had gotten possession of that See : and then he wrote to the Emperor, and requested that he would banish Peter from Antioch and the neighbourhood. In his letter, or sentence, sent to Peter the Fuller, he asserts that *absolute power was given to S. Peter,* and that *Rome is the head of the whole Church.*

t Ep. l. Mansi, vii. c. 1028.   Certe si, &c. and c. 1030.

u Ibid. c. 1032. 1036.

x Ibid. c. 1048. 1049.

But Felix soon went farther than this. After having in vain summoned Acacius before him to take his trial, on July 28, 484, he wrote and published in a Synod at Rome, where it was subscribed by sixty-seven Bishops, a formal sentence of deposition and excommunication upon him.

The first offence alleged in this decree is[y], the invasion of the provinces of other Bishops; which means, the patriarchal authority given to the See of Constantinople by the Council of Chalcedon; after this come, the holding communion with condemned heretics, and promoting them; especially the holding communion with Peter Mongus, and allowing him to occupy the See of Alexandria, to the exclusion of the Bishop lawfully elected (i. e. John, who had fled to Rome, and against whom the other side brought accusations); the ill-treatment, and finally, the corrupting by bribes of the late Legates sent from Rome, to the damage of S. Peter (*in læsionem b. P. apostoli*); the refusal to come to Rome to be tried

---

[y] Mansi, vii. c. 1054. Comp. the Letter in c. 1067.

according to the Canons, meaning those of *Sar-dica* (which gave *no such power*) ; and the neglect of the Pope's Envoy or Nuncio sent to require this, so as not even to admit him to an interview. For these things the Pope condemned Acacius, as above described.

Here we find the *appellate jurisdiction* given by the Sardican Canons, i. e. the power to receive and try appeals when made, turned into a *coactive jurisdiction ;* and a right pretended to summon all persons, and try all ecclesiastical causes *ex officio,* on the authority of those Canons, which contain nothing concerning such a power.

Acacius' conduct does seem open to blame for inconsistency in his intercourse with the schis-matical party. He had first opposed Peter Mon-gus, as an intruder and disturber of the Church of Alexandria [z] : afterwards, when on the next vacancy he got possession of the See, and was allowed by the Emperor, Acacius was in commu-nion with him. But it is expressly said, that Peter, who was an artful unscrupulous man, gave

[z] Mansi, c. 982.

- the fullest assurance of his orthodoxy to Acacius, when he required satisfaction on that point, although it is related that this was really a deceit, and that Acacius was imposed upon[a].

Acacius was accused by some of his adversaries of truckling to the Court in the question. The Emperor Zeno did not favour the Council of Chalcedon, certainly : but neither would he allow Bishops to condemn it and decry its authority : and there seems to be satisfactory evidence, that Acacius never joined nor assented in any way to those who openly condemned that Council: [b]the soundness of his faith and morals in private life is attested by Pope Anastasius II. How far he might have been compliant to the sentiments prevailing at Court, and how far he might have been moved by the desire of peace and charity, or by any personal reason, it is impossible now for us to determine : the chief part

---

[a] Evagr. iii. 17, 18.
[b] Epist. ad Anast. Imper. Mansi, viii. c. 188.

of the information which we have on the subject is from the Roman side. Certainly there were objections made against the candidate for the See of Alexandria, whose cause the Pope espoused: so that Acacius had some ground for not assenting to the Pope's demand on this head; although there is not enough recorded of particulars for us to judge of the validity of the reasons.

And Acacius had good ground for resisting the Pope's arbitrary claims of authority as supreme judge in the question. When summoned to Rome to take his trial, in obedience to the Canon of Sardica under the name of Nicæa, he could not but treat the demand with contempt. If it was not the case, that the measures which the Pope proposed with regard to the various questions in debate were so violent and extreme that he could not concur in them, (which is possible) at least the extravagant pretensions of personal authority in the successor of S. Peter over the Church of Constantinople, and the whole of the East, left him no liberty of choice: if he submitted, he sanctioned a false pretence; if he resisted, he was condemned as the friend of heretics.

The doctrine of the Supremacy of Rome was now fully "developed." Pope Felix, having gone so far, carried it out consistently in the rest of his proceedings. Some of the Monks at Constantinople seem to have been much in the Pope's confidence, his agents indeed, or at least supporters, against their own Patriarch[c]. After the condemnation of Acacius, Felix wrote to a principal Abbot at Constantinople, desiring him to hold no communication with Acacius, except by his order[d]. He wrote also to the body of Abbots and Monks, desiring them to punish their own members who adhered to Acacius[e]: and in a Synod of forty-two Bishops[f], addressed a letter

---

[c] See what Evagrius says of Cyril, H. E. iii. 18 and 19, and of Symeon, 21. This was the Monastery of the Ἀκοίμηται.

[d] Mansi, vii. c. 1103.

[e] Ibid. c. 1068.

[f] Ibid. c. 1142. Pagi speaks of this and the Synod of sixty-seven Bishops as two Synods and two sentences on Acacius. But the second Synod would hardly *repeat* the sentence of the first, although the (fresh) question of Antioch was the reason for its meeting. It rather (I think) considers Acacius as

to the Clergy and Monks of the East, informing them of what had been done against Acacius, and requiring them to concur in it [g].

He also wrote to the Emperor Zeno to the same effect, asking for his approval and assistance [h].

In all these the Supremacy of Rome is stated more or less clearly. In the letter to the Emperor, we find for the first time the phrase, which afterwards was so notorious. He says, "[i] *S. Peter the Apostle speaks in mé his Vicar*," and "*Christ speaks in him.*" Thus, at last, it was declared explicitly, that the Pope is the Vicar of the Apostle, in whom Christ speaks: and the transition was easy from this to the shorter equivalent, *The Pope is Christ's Vicar*. When this doctrine was admitted, all the rest followed.

Acacius died soon after this, A.D. 489 [k]. His

already condemned, and asks for assent to the former sentence; setting forth on this occasion that very strong statement of the Supremacy in "Quotiens intra Italiam, &c." c. 1140.

[g] Mansi, c. 1139.

[h] Ibid. c. 1097.

[i] Ibid. c. 1099. In c. 1098, he claims "the Keys" to S. Peter, &c.

[k] Fast. Roman. Append. p. 559.

successor Flavitas or Fravitas, upon his appointment addressed a letter of compliment to the Pope, as usual. The Pope acknowledged it by an answer in friendly terms. Fravitas' letter is not extant : the Pope, in his answer, states[1] the Roman Supremacy in very full terms, that "*Christ gave to the Apostolic seat power to confirm the dignity of all priests, &c. ;*" all which, he says, that Fravitas acknowledged in his letter : and he quotes the testimony of the Monks (who were his supporters) in favour of Fravitas. So that it seems clear that Fravitas did submit to the claims of Rome, to a certain extent, at least in words. But the Pope required that the names of both Peter Mongus and Acacius should be erased from the diptychs, or register of the Bishops of the Church : which was not conceded. Fravitas, however, died after a few[m] months, A.D. 490; and the breach was not healed. Facundus tells us,

---

[1] Mansi, vii. c. 1100, &c.

[m] He lived four months, according to Evagr. iii. 23. Theophanes and other writers say three months. See Fast. Rom. Append. p. 559.

that all the East, except a few Churches, re-mained out of communion with Rome for forty years [n].

We have now traced the growth of the power of Rome from the first overt act of building it up into a system at Sardica, to the establishment of it by a sentence enforced, which, whether right or wrong, became a precedent, and made the world familiar with the idea at least of Roman Supremacy.

[n] Contra Mocian. p. 200.

LECTURE III.

PART I.

POPE GELASIUS, who succeeded Felix II, A.D. 492, did not deviate from the course of his predecessors; the power of the Supremacy continued to advance. In the contest with Constantinople, he relaxed nothing of the Roman claim. He exchanged letters at first on friendly terms with Euphemius the Patriarch (A.D. 490): but as he insisted upon the rejection of Acacius' name from the register of the Church, and his condemnation as a heretic, and Euphemius would not consent to this, the two Churches remained separate as before.

Meanwhile there was a considerable discussion of arguments: beside a letter to Euphemius, Gelasius wrote also to the Illyrian Bishops, to the

Emperor Anastasius, to the Oriental Bishops, and to some other persons, letters or treatises (some of them circulars) of various lengths, on the "Acacian question," which are extant. The matter and style of some of these exhibit the policy and principles of his government, and mark the progress of Papal development.

He takes to his own See, throughout, the title *Apostolic:* "the Apostolic Chair" is the distinction of Rome, meaning the seat of S. Peter, and the authority claimed in his name.

He asserts the *principatus,* which the Lord gave to S. Peter, which the Church (he says) has preserved ever since[a]: *the chief government (gubernatio principalis) of the whole Church, &c.* that, according to the Canons, Rome has *authority*[b] *to receive and try all cases of appeals* made to her (i. e. the Canons of Sardica again) : that all *can appeal to Rome, but none from Rome;* and that Rome has power *to revoke any and every judgment given by any other authority in the*

---

[a] Mansi, viii. c. 51, 65, 48, 34, A.

[b] Ibid. c. 53, 54.

Church[c]*:* that Rome can *judge the whole Church,*
but can *not be judged by any one*[d], but *all must obey
her* sentence : that by the Canons[e] (i. e. of Sardica
again) none *but Rome has supreme jurisdiction ;*
but even the Sardican Canons gave no jurisdiction, except in appeals : he asserts, that *what
Rome approves and confirms has authority,* without
this confirmation nothing has authority[f] *;* which
amounts to saying, that every Council must wait
for the Pope to ratify its acts before they can be
valid, contrary to what Pope Innocentius the
First had said.   He asserts, that the Pope has
authority to relax and modify, that is, to change,
ancient canons or customs to suit present circumstances, contrary to what Pope Leo had said
of the Nicene Canons.   According to these principles, he says, that the Council of Chalcedon
has authority according to Scripture, tradition,
and the Canons, &c. *so far as Rome sanctioned*

---

c Mansi, c. 54.
d Ibid. c. 17. D.
e Ibid. c. 19. C.
f Ibid. c. 51. D. c. 88. c. 92. C. (especially).

H

what was there decreed: what Rome did not approve, ought not to be received by the Church ᵍ.
And he also asserts a *general obligation on the
whole Church to follow the order of Rome in everything* ʰ.

In writing to the Emperor Anastasius, whom
he reproves rather unceremoniously, he tells
him, there are two powers which govern the
world, the *sacred authority of the Pontiffs,* (*auctoritas sacra Pontificum*) and *the royal power*
(*regalis potestas*) : and as he names the Pontifical
government first, so he goes on to shew why,
for many reasons, the Priest is superior to the
King ⁱ.

ᵍ Mansi, c. 88. To this he adds a sophism for an argument by
analogy : The other erroneous decisions of the Council, he says,
are not more to be received than the evil deeds recorded in
Scripture are to be imitated, &c.—as if Scripture had ever
mentioned any evil *as a rule to be followed,* in the same manner
in which it gives precepts to obey! Whereas the Council set
forth that which the Pope disliked, as a rule having authority,
pro gradu suo, from the same source as those things which the
Pope received, viz. the consent of the Council.

ʰ Ibid. c. 40.

ⁱ Ibid. c. 31. In his Circular he resumes this subject,

Thus was first broached this great principle, which was afterwards made so instrumental to the establishing of that sovereignty over all the temporal powers, which the Pope at one time exercised.

In the discussion about Acacius, the Pope repeatedly sneered at Constantinople for being only a Diocese of the province of Heraclea [k], not even a Metropolitan See, still less a Patriarchal one, and not of Apostolic foundation; and he ridiculed the idea of rank belonging to it because it was the imperial city [l].

The troubled state of the Western Empire caused Gelasius to be often consulted by provincial Bishops and Clergy on Church business: and he had often to interpose for the correction of wrongs or disorders [m].

carrying it back to Melchisedech, &c. placing the two divine institutions, the spiritual and the temporal sovereignty, quite on a parallel footing. He infers from this, that no Prince can condemn a Bishop, &c. c. 93, and see Binius' note at the end.

[k] Mansi, c. 53, 54.

[l] Ibid. c. 58.

[m] Ibid. c. 123, &c. c. 37, &c.

He sent a Nuncio to the Bishops of Illyria at their request [n]; he wrote to Honorius, Bishop of Dalmatia, against the Pelagians, somewhat to his surprise at the interference, which the Pope excused on the plea of a duty to watch over all Churches [o].

He renewed correspondence with the Bishop of Arles [p], which had been broken off apparently by the dispute about the Metropolitan authority there.

He sent Decrees or Canons to some of the provinces; among which was an order to the Lucanian Bishops, that *no Church should be consecrated without leave from Rome* [q].

A Council at Rome of seventy Bishops under him, A. D. 494, treated of important matters, ending in nothing less than a Decree to settle the whole Canon of Scripture, and the authority of the Councils and Fathers, and to reject apo-

[n] Mansi, c. 13.   He wrote again to them a long treatise, &c. c. 49 and 46.

[o] Ibid. c. 22, and the foregoing epistle.

[p] Ibid. c. 48.

[q] Ad Episcopos Lucaniæ, &c. c. 38 and 44.

cryphal or erroneous books. It sets forth all these things as follows[r]. First, the names of the Canonical Books of Scripture; among which are reckoned, The Wisdom of Solomon, Ecclesiasticus, the Book of Tobit, Judith, and the two Books of Maccabees: but the Revelations are omitted. This forms the first Article or Canon.

The second is a remarkable one; and as it bears closely.upon the present subject of inquiry, I will give it literally.

"After all these prophetical, evangelical, and apostolic Scriptures, on which the Catholic Church is by the grace of God built, we think it right to state also, that although there is one bridal chamber of Christ for the Catholic Church throughout the world, yet the holy Roman Catholic and Apostolic Church is set above other Churches by no Synodical Constitutions, but has obtained the primacy by the evangelical word of our Lord and Saviour, who said, *Thou art Peter, and upon this*

---

[r] Mansi, viii. c. 145. [But Pearson, Vind. Ign. p. 45, ed. Cant. 1672, and Cave, &c. reject this Council as spurious: Pagi defends it, but places it in A. D. 496.]

rock I will build my Church, and the gates of hell shall not prevail against it. And I will give unto thee the keys of the kingdom of heaven: and whatsoever thou shalt bind on earth shall be bound also in heaven, and whatsoever thou shalt loose on earth shall be loosed also in heaven.

" To whom was given also the fellowship of Saint Paul, that chosen vessel, who, not at a different time, as the heretics babble, but at the same time, in the same day, with Peter was crowned by a glorious death in the city of Rome, suffering under Cæsar Nero; and together they consecrated the aforesaid holy Roman Church to Christ the Lord, and as such set it above all cities in the whole world, by their presence and admirable (*venerando*) triumph.

" Therefore the Roman Church, the seat of the Apostle Peter, is the first, *not having spot, nor wrinkle, nor any such thing.*

" But the second seat was consecrated at Alexandria, in the name of S. Peter, by his disciple and evangelist Mark: who himself, sent

into Egypt by the Apostle Peter, preached the
word of truth, and accomplished a glorious mar-
tyrdom (testimony) *martyrium.*

" But the third seat at Antioch is held in
honour in the name of the same Apostle S. Peter;
because he dwelt there before he came to Rome,
and there the name of the new nation, the
Christians, first arose."

Here we see there is no mention made of the
most ancient, primitive, and Apostolic See of
Jerusalem; nor of Constantinople, to which rank
in the Church had been given by two General
Councils. Neither of these two contributed
anything to increase the honour claimed for
S. Peter's name : but both, Jerusalem by her
independence, and Constantinople by her opposition, bore testimony against the pretended *Supremacy.*

It would have been difficult for Pope Gelasius
to prove two things which he asserted here, viz.
that S. Mark was *sent into Egypt by S. Peter,* and
that, when he founded the Alexandrian Church,

he did it in S. Peter's name. The early traditions say nothing of either of these two
points [s].

It might be justly argued also, that here Rome
bears witness against herself even in the dignity
which she allows to these two (only) Patriarch-
ates. Because the Roman precedence was *such
in kind as theirs* was, and *no more.* As they had
dignity on account of antiquity, custom, eminence,
consent of the Church, and similar reasons, so
also had Rome for *the same reasons.* If Rome
had really possessed by divine right the *government* of the Church, (which was the assumed
Supremacy) the distance in rank between her
and Alexandria or Antioch would have been too

---

[s] Euseb. H. E. ii. 16, who gives the ancient tradition, that
S. Mark was the founder of the Alexandrian Church. As for
the rest of the particulars added to this in later times, Renaudot
observes, that the same account (Severus') which reports that
S. Mark was *sent by S. Peter,* says also, in direct contradiction
to this, that the Apostles drew lots for the countries to which
each should go and preach, and that Alexandria *fell by lot to
S. Mark.* One of these stories is just *as trustworthy* as the
other. Renaudot, Hist. Patriarch. Alexandr. p. 3.

great for these to be consistently reckoned "*second*" and "*third*," as if in the same rank, when they were really *subject Churches.*

Then the Decree proceeds, and mentions the four General Councils by name, which are introduced thus :—

"And, although no one can lay *any other foundation than that is laid,* which is Christ Jesus, yet for our edification the same holy Roman Church does not forbid these writings (Scriptures) to be received also after the Holy Scriptures of the Old and New Testaments, namely, the holy Council of Nicæa, &c.——:" after which the other three General Councils are named, (but the Council of Constantinople is omitted in two MSS. out of the three[t]) and a clause is added, including generally other Councils of the Fathers in the second place.

The form of expression here runs as if all the Councils received their authority from the

---

[t] Mansi, viii. c. 159.

sanction of Rome, rather than furnished any rule for Rome to follow.

Then are enumerated by name the works of several Fathers, beginning with S. Cyprian; and also of all those in general who have in nothing deviated from the Roman Communion: also the Decretal Epistles of all the Popes.

After these, the Acts of the Martyrs, Legends of the Saints, and some other works of doubtful authority, are named, which, they say, are to be received with all honour, and may be read according to S. Paul's direction, *Prove all things, hold fast that which is good.*

And lastly, there is a long list of apocryphal works, which are not to be received: which ends with a catalogue of heretics, who are to be rejected and condemned.

This Decree, beside its general importance, had also a particular effect on some of the controversies of that time. For among the books condemned as apocryphal or unsound, were the works of some of the principal Semi-pelagians, as Cassianus, and Faustus; while S. Augustine, the great authority for the doctrine concerning grace, the active opponent of the Pelagians, and after his death the passive object of the opposition of the Semi-pelagians, was reckoned among the Fathers of the Church, whose works are to be received for orthodox.

Pope Gelasius filled the Chair but little more than four years and a half; but they were active years for the Papal influence: you have seen from his acts and writings what that influence had now grown to. The principles which he expressed and acted upon had now so firmly established themselves, that they were generally recognised and allowed in the West, though rejected by the Eastern Church; they were now the received system of the Papal government in the Church: and there will be no need to point them out afresh, whenever they may be repeated formally from time to time as we proceed on-wards, but only the additions made to them, or any other peculiarity.

I am unwilling to omit here one little notice,

because, although not important in the subject matter, it furnishes a characteristic trait of the age. In a Council at Rome, A. D. 495, Misenus, one of the Legates who had been excommunicated for his conduct in the controversy with Acacius at Constantinople, begged for absolution from this sentence. When his petition had been read, the Pope asked the Council what they wished to be done: on which the report in the Acta proceeds thus [u]. "All the Bishops and Presbyters rose up and entreated him, saying, O Christ, hear. Long life to Gelasius: repeated twenty times. Perform what God has given into your power: repeated twelve times. Do that which Lord Peter does: repeated ten times. We

---

[u] "Levaverunt se omnes episcopi et presbyteri, rogantes et . dicentes, Exaudi, Christe: Gelasio vita: dictum vicies. Quod vobis Deus dedit in potestate, præstate: dictum duodecies. Hoc fac quod facit dominus Petrus: dictum decies. Ut indulgeas rogamus: dictum novies," &c. Mansi, viii. c. 180. This form was kept up by Popes in later ages. The Council of Trent closed their proceedings with something of the same kind, but in better taste, under the title, *Acclamationes Patrum in Fine Concilii.* See Conc. Trid. Can. et Decr.

entreat you to shew favour : repeated nine times, &c."

This shews how the style of address to a Pope had been changed since the days of S. Jerome; who, about 120 years before this, wrote to Pope Damasus at the beginning of one of his letters in the terms quoted above, p. 22ᵛ.

The next Pope, Anastasius II. sat for a short time only, from Nov. 24, 496, to Nov. 17, 498 : but that time is distinguished by one great event, the Baptism of Clovis, King of the Franks, A. D. 496, (to whom Anastasius wrote a letter of congratulation on the subject[x]) as well as by the different turn which this Pope endeavoured to give to the question at issue between Rome and Constantinople.

Anastasius, the then reigning Emperor, was opposed to the Council of Chalcedon : and the Eutychian party from Alexandria, where the Bishop, Athanasius, had received the Henoticon

---

[v] Hieron. Ep. xvi. 2.

[x] Mansi, viii. c. 193.

of the Emperor Zeno, applied to him to use his influence to induce the Pope to receive them into communion. The Pope wrote to the Emperor a letter y, the principal part of the little that now exists of the writings of Pope Anastasius II, in which he mentioned the " cause of the Alexandrians," and prayed the Emperor to endeavour to bring them to a sounder faith.

But the main subject of this letter was the old " Acacian question," now of twelve years' standing, which the Pope endeavoured to settle. He begged the Emperor to order, that the name of Acacius should be simply omitted in the public reading of the Register of the Bishops, in order to avoid the dissensions which the mention of it excited: but he offered to allow all the ministerial acts of Acacius, namely, the validity of all ordinations or baptisms performed by him.

The omission of his name alone was of course a censure upon Acacius: and the Pope accordingly sent with this letter Legates, to whom he

---

y Mansi, c. 188, &c.

referred the Emperor for evidence [z] of Acacius' irregularities, (while he admitted his virtues in private life) which justified the Pope in making such a demand.

But the allowing his ordinations and other acts to be valid, proves that the Pope did not consider Acacius as cut off from the body of the Church. For Binius' explanations [a] of this, that the Pope did it by his dispensing power, is inconsistent with the arguments which he used in his letter to shew why it ought to be so : since he condemned the mistake of those, who thought that the sentence of Pope Felix made all the sacramental acts of Acacius from that time null and void.

This negotiation produced no good result. Meanwhile another messenger from Rome, a Senator, (Festus) sent on some secular business, offered to gratify the Emperor by persuading the Pope to subscribe to the Henoticon of the Emperor Zeno ; his offer was accepted, and,

[z] Mansi, c. 189.
[a] Note c, c. 192.

charged with this mission, he returned from Constantinople to Rome: but the Pope escaped this
trial by death; when Festus returned, the Chair
was vacant [b]. Anastasius' peacemaking overture
concerning Acacius did not heal the breach with
Constantinople. His letter to the Emperor is
remarkable for the moderate tone in which it is
written, compared with those of some of his predecessors.

When Symmachus was elected in Nov. 498,
in the Church of Constantine [c], Laurentius was
elected by an opposition party in S. Mary's
Church, through the intrigues, it is said, of the
same Senator Festus [d]. The Clergy and the
people were divided on the question: and it was
referred to Theodoric, the Gothic King, who was
then at Ravenna.

He gave his judgment in favour of Symmachus, who was thereupon acknowledged for Pope;

[b] Theodor. Lect. ii. 17. Niceph. xvi. 35.

[c] Lib. Pontifical. in Mansi, viii. c. 201. Anastas. Vit. Pontif. i.
p. 85. ed. Rom. 1718.

[d] Theodor. Lect. ii. 17.

and in the following year, on the first of March, presided over a Synod at Rome [e], in which three severe Canons were made against intriguing for the Papacy.

All of the Clergy, who, in the lifetime of a Pope, pledged themselves, or promised their support in any way, to one who would be a candidate to succeed him, and likewise any one who canvassed for this object, were to be deposed from all office or degree in the Church : he, whom the majority of the Clergy should elect, was to be Pope on every vacancy, unless the late Pope had decreed who should succeed him (which shews that it was partly contemplated now to make the Papacy in this way hereditary). And all who gave information, so as to convict persons offending against this Canon concerning intriguing and canvassing, were to be rewarded by preferment. This indicates the manner in which (as we may suppose) the party of Laurentius had managed his election.

---

[e] Mansi, viii. c. 229, and Pagi, A. D. 499.

I

In the same Synod[f] the Pope got rid of his rival, by appointing him to be Bishop of Nuceria.

Thus, for the present, peace was restored: but it did not last long[g]. The Laurentian party brought accusations against the Pope; Laurentius was secretly brought back to Rome; and the matter was again referred to King Theodoric: it seems the opposing party, about Easter A. D. 501[h], carried their complaints against Symmachus to him. Both the Senate and the Clergy petitioned him to call a Council[i], and they also asked him to appoint Peter, Bishop of Altina, Visitor of the See of Rome; a new (and certainly *not a canonical*) office, by which a Bishop was to have authority under the King's commission to try the Pope. Theodoric granted both;

[f] Lib. Pontifical. in Mansi, viii. c. 201. Anastas. Vit. Pontif. i. p. 85.

[g] The Lib. Pontif. says, after four years the schism was renewed. In what follows, the space is reckoned from Nov. 498, to Easter 501.

[h] Fragm. in Mansi, viii. c. 204. Precept. Reg. c. 256, and note, c. 303, &c.

[i] See the Præceptio in Mansi, c. 254, E.

he appointed Peter of Altina Visitor, and summoned a Council to meet at Rome : but the first summons had no effect towards deciding the question.

The Bishops met and began to consider the question soon after Easter.

Some[j] objections which had been raised, on the ground that it was summoned by the King and not by the Pope, were removed by the Pope himself : for he appeared at the opening of the business, and expressed his obligation to the King for having called it.

The Council then proposed[k] to restore the Pope to his former condition, by recovering to him all the patrimony, estates, churches, &c. of which he had been deprived by the opposing party, or in consequence of the contest now in progress : they wished to effect this by a formal Synodical sentence, before they proceeded to examine the accusations brought against him ; but as they did not venture to decide this point with-

[j] Mansi, viii. c. 247, &c.
[k] Ibid. c. 249.

out the consent of the King, they sent to him before they made a decree; and his answer was unfavourable to their wishes. He said, the Pope must first answer to the charges brought against him, before he could have possession of the rights of his See.

They therefore took this subject in hand to examine: and the Pope was coming to the Council to plead, when he was attacked by the opposing party, his attendants were ill treated, and he was obliged to flee.

After this, he refused to come again before the Council: and when summoned formally four times, he answered, that he had been willing, at the King's request, to waive his privilege, and submit to the judgment of the Council; but that since he and his Clergy had been so cruelly used in going thither, he could not after that submit to any trial by them.

The proceedings of the Council were therefore stopped. And[1] they broke up the meeting, and

---

[1] Mansi, c. 250, compared with the Præceptio per Germanum, &c. c. 253, 254.

again sent to the King. The Bishops seem to have been afraid of the opposing party; especially as not all of those who had been summoned had arrived[m] : and they wished the King to call the Council to Ravenna, where he was living, or else come himself to the Council at Rome. But he refused to call them to Ravenna, alleging the inconvenience to which that would put some of the Bishops.

The end was, that in a letter dated Aug. 8, he renewed his order for the same number of Bishops, as had been already summoned, to meet again at Rome on Sept. 1, 501[n], and there to give judgment on the case, which should be final : and he added, that if this were not done, he would come himself to Rome, and take his own measures for restoring peace to the city. He was an Arian.

His letter of Aug. 8, addressed to the Bishops of the Council at Rome, was followed by another order to the same effect, more strongly expressed,

---

[m] Præceptio per Germanum. Mansi, c. 254.
[n] Mansi, c. 254.

sent to the Council through the Mayor of the Palace, dated Aug. 27°.

Still it seems the business lingered, on account of the Pope's refusal to attend. He said, " I came to your first meeting, when you assembled in Rome, without hesitation, &c.; when I was coming again, I was cruelly ill treated;" and he said he would come no more.

The Council therefore again sent a memorial to the King, (in which they acknowledged the receipt of the King's command by the Mayor of the Palace) stating their difficulty, because they have no power to compel the Pope, who has by the Canons supreme power over all Bishops. And, in conclusion, they prayed for leave to go home to their dioceses [p].

The King did not consent to this, but required them to go on with the business for which they had been called together, and to bring it to a conclusion.

o Mansi, c. 254, 255, 256.
p Ibid. c. 256.

His answer to the Council is dated Oct. 1. In it he said[q], "He wondered that they had again consulted him, when he had expressly directed them to examine and decide the case; that he with his nobles might have examined it for himself, and with God's help have determined what was just; so that none should have had reason to blame his judgment; but that because he thought it was not for him to judge questions belonging to the Church, therefore he had called a Council, that they might, in the fear of God, decide what was right;" and, in conclusion, he declared he would leave the question entirely to their discretion, but he required them peremptorily to give a judgment on the case. Another[r] letter of similar import was addressed to the Council through his Secretary. This manly and equitable command of the Arian Prince had effect: and the Synod gave sentence, by fully acquitting Pope Symmachus of all the charges

[q] Mansi, c. 257, 258.
[r] Ibid.

against him, and declaring him the lawful pos-
sessor of all the rights and privileges of the
Papacy. October 23, 501.

It is to be observed, that this sentence was
given with a clause of reservation in it: viz. it
was expressed, "so far as concerns man; because,
for the reasons above noticed, it is plain that the
whole [accusation] was dismissed by the divine
judgment:" (*quantum ad homines respicit; quia
totum, causis obsistentibus superius designatis, con-
stat arbitrio divino fuisse dismissum*) which
evidently relates to the question between the
ecclesiastical and the secular authority; perhaps more particularly to the sentence in the
Pope's favour which the Council wished to give,
before they should examine the accusations
against him, and which Theodoric would not
permit.

The authority of the Visitor of the Church of
Rome, Peter of Altina, seems to have been quite
excluded in this Council: no notice of him
appears in the report of the proceedings, except
an allusion in the form of a protest against his

intrusion [s]. It is said on good authority [t], that he was condemned in a Synod. But it is not certain in which. Laurentius the Antipope was anathematized also.

We have now had three Councils on this question, one A.D. 499, two in A.D. 501. There was a fourth, and also a fifth, and even a sixth, upon the same subject. But the chronology is obscure, and has been the cause of much discussion: Pagi disputed Baronius' calculations, and has himself been corrected by Mansi. I have followed the order of events, which may be traced by comparison of the authentic accounts: and so far as this I think it is clear enough.

The next Council after this was probably that which was called (from the place where it met) Palmaris, A.D. 502, in which perhaps the decision of the foregoing Synod might have been confirmed: for the former Decrees are alluded to,

[s] Mansi, c. 249, A.

[t] Anastas. Vit. Symm. and Mansi, viii. c. 201. The same appears from the Letter of John the Deacon, in Mansi, c. 344, which shews that both Peter and Laurentius were anathematized.

and approved by the Pope. But it is chiefly remarkable for another cause.

In it the law of Odoacer, that no Pope should
be elected without the consent of the King[n], was
annulled, and set aside as invalid, because it was
not confirmed by the Pope's subscription, nor by
any ecclesiastical authority; and no layman, they
said, had authority to legislate on any Church
matters.

Another law of the same King, prohibiting for
ever all alienation of any property belonging to
the Church, under pain of an anathema, was
also set aside for the same reason. But at the
Pope's request the Council agreed to confirm
this : and the Pope proceeded to decree five
Canons on this point, which the Council adopted,
to the same effect as King Odoacer's law against
alienations.

The fifth Council, in 503[x], decreed, that all
the Bishops who had been deprived of any benefices during the late contests should receive them
again.

<hr/>

[n] See above, page 80.   [x] Mansi, viii. c. 295.

The sixth Council[y], on October 1, was not directly concerned with the schism of Laurentius, but bore upon matters which grew out of it, which shew the state of the times then. It was against the invasion of the property of the Church: and it decreed, that all who confiscated or appropriated that which belonged to the Church, should be for ever under an anathema. There is a decree[z] of King Theodoric's following up this sentence, by forbidding all alienations, dated Ravenna, A. D. 507, March 11. Probably the Council was not long before this : perhaps A. D. 506.

The decision of the case in the Pope's favour, in the third Council, was not received in silence by his adversaries. A book was published by them against the judgment, either of the third or the fourth Council, with the title, "Against the Council of the Doubtful Acquittal" (*Adversus Synodum absolutionis incertæ*).

This at the command of the Pope and Council

---

[y] Mansi, viii. c. 309.
[z] Ibid. c. 345.

was answered by a writer of reputation at that time, Ennodius, Bishop of Ticinum : and his work was afterwards adopted and authorized by the fifth Council, and ordered to be inserted before the Acta of the fourth and fifth Councils [a].

Ennodius, in a tone of haughty reproof of his opponents, maintains in the broadest terms the doctrines of the Papal supremacy.

The adverse party had greatly blamed the Council, for saying that the Pope ought to call a Council, not the King; and they argued, that the doctrine that the Pope was superior to every tribunal, was in fact allowing an immunity to do wrong to the successors of S. Peter.

To this Ennodius replied, that *S. Peter bequeathed his own merits to his successors*, as well as his authority. " For who," he says, " can doubt the sanctity of one raised to such a height of dignity? in whom, if there is a lack of goodness acquired by his own merits, *that which his predecessors bestow is enough :* for it (the dignity) either raises up illustrious men,

[a] Synod. Rom. v. Mansi, viii. c. 295.

or else makes those illustrious who are raised by it [b]."

This asserts the Pope to be impeccable, as well as infallible, by virtue of his office, and might without difficulty be stretched to cover all irregularities, even personal vices of Popes, by this application of "the merits of his predecessors."

The opposition said, that the Pope was bound to plead to the accusations against him before the King; which Ennodius regards as a monstrous assertion. And to the objection, that the Pope by coming before the Council, as he did, to answer, shewed there was no force in the plea, that no Pope ever had been tried, Ennodius replies by quoting from Isaiah, *Shall the axe boast itself against him that heweth therewith* [c]? &c.

[b] Ille (Petrus) perennem meritorum dotem cum hæreditate innocentiæ misit ad posteros : quod illi concessum est pro actqum luce, ad illos pertinet, quos par conversationis splendor illuminat. Quis enim sanctum esse dubitet quem apex tantæ dignitatis attollit, in quo si *desint bona acquisita per meritum, sufficiunt quæ a loci decessore præstantur?* aut enim claros ad hæc fastigia erigit, aut qui eriguntur illustrat. Mansi, viii. c. 275.

[c] Is. x. 15. Ennod. in Mansi, viii. c. 276.

Ennodius quotes the Canon of Sardica to prove, that no judgment of a Council can stand against the Pope's authority, since he is the final Court of Appeal[d]: and says, that God, who designed that the causes of other men should be tried by men, has reserved the judging of S. Peter's successors to himself, without question[e].

The case therefore remained as a contested precedent on the question of right, like those former instances of Boniface I, and Sextus III; indeed, the opposing party now quoted the case of Boniface and the Antipope Eulalius, to prove that the Pope might be tried: that is to say, the Pope did in fact appear, and his case was tried, in a Council called under the King's authority, but he did it under a protest, that it was his own voluntary act; and his party asserted, that his authority was really above that of his judge.

Nevertheless, it gave occasion to the further development and progress of the extreme opinions

d C. 282.   e C. 284.

concerning the Pope's supremacy and immunity;. and there can be little doubt, that the result was favourable to the actual power of the See. The minds of men were more accustomed to the idea, that the Pope was above all human authority.

This appears in a letter from the Bishops of France, headed by Avitus [f], Archbishop of Vienne, addressed to some Senators at Rome, on the subject of the late proceedings against the Pope; in which they express their fear of all encroachment on his divine prerogative, and deny that he can be called to account, or judged.

The account which we have of these proceedings is almost all from Symmachus' side of the question: there is only a fragment of a life of him from a writer of the opposite party [g], which gives a different turn to some things. From this we learn, that the Pope was accused of bribery, (a common charge from rivals) irregularity of some kind with women, and alienating the pro-

[f] Mansi, viii. c. 293.
[g] Ibid. c. 203.

perty of the Church. Symmachus alluded to the last as a calumny of his enemies, when he decreed the Canon prohibiting all alienations in the fourth Council.

The same writer says also, that after the schism was renewed by the accusations against Symmachus, the King made him for a while reside at Ariminum. And that Laurentius left Nuceria, and came to Rome, and resided there for about four years, during which there were great contests, with fighting and bloodshed : until the King ordered that all the property of the Church should be given up to Symmachus. On which, Laurentius retired to an estate belonging to his supporter, the Patrician Festus, where he died.[h].

This order of the King might have been the effect of the decree of the sixth Council, that all invaders of Church property should incur an anathema.

[h] The anonymous fragment in Mansi, viii. c. 203, says four years. Theodorus Lector. says they disputed for three years.

Symmachus corresponded with Æonius, Bishop of Arles, again about the old question of the Metropolitan authority[i]. Æonius had consulted Pope Gelasius (as was said above, p. 100) upon this business: what that Pope had directed to be done does not appear: but his successor, Anastasius II, had made some regulations, in consequence of which a dispute had arisen between the Bishops of Arles and of Vienne, about consecrating their Suffragans.

Symmachus now decreed, that Anastasius' regulation should be set aside as an innovation, which threw the provinces into confusion; and that the order settled by Pope Leo I. should be restored[k]. His language on this subject concerning the authority of the Papal decrees is curious.

He says, " For while the Bishop's (Pope's) office is one and the same in different Bishops, like the Trinity, whose power is one and undivided,

---

[i] Symmach. Ep. i. ii. v. &c. in Mansi, viii. c. 208.

[k] Symmach. Ep. ix. c. 226.

how is it right that the statutes of former Popes
should be broken by their successors? Moreover,
we believe it to be a property of the holy Catholic
religion to have no differences of opinion : of
which the whole power is weakened, unless all
things ordained by the Priests of the Lord be
perpetual."—" For *what respect will be thought due
to the vicegerents of the holy Apostle S. Peter, if
what they ordain while they are in the See, be undone
as soon as they have quitted it*[1]?"

This is the more remarkable, when we remember what former Popes had decreed about Arles.
Zosimus made a new regulation, professing in
that to restore the rightful primitive custom of
Apostolic times : Popes Bonifacius, Cælestinus,
and Leo I. condemned this, and set it aside. Leo
called it a temporary arrangement, and by a
decree of his own, ordered that Arles should be
subject to Vienne; and then, after a few years,
ordered something different, which was a kind of

---

[1] Mansi, viii. c. 208.

compromise between the two claims [m]. Anastasius had changed this again: and now Symmachus revoked Anastasius' acts, on the ground, that all the ordinances of S. Peter's chair must be perpetual and unchangeable.

We may see here, as in some other instances, how Rome advanced in the loftiness of her language, and the severity of her professions, in proportion as the state of things in the Church grew really worse, and her practice became more visibly inconsistent.

The Emperor Anastasius was adverse to the Council of Chalcedon: he favoured the Bishops who condemned it, and oppressed those who supported it; and he favoured the cause of Acacius. The Pope, with the concurrence of the Roman senate, excommunicated him [n]. He in return published an invective against the Pope.

[m] After Leo, Hilarus had given a decree inhibiting the Bishop of Narbonne from exercising Metropolitan authority. But there is no proof that this was any *change*. Mansi, vii. c. 934.

[n] Mansi, viii. c. 215.

Neither of these writings exists : but the Pope's answer is preserved.   In it the Pope draws a comparison between the Emperor's authority and his own : *" But let us compare the honour of the Emperor with the honour of the Pontiff : between whom there is this difference, that the former has the care of human things, the latter of divine things* [o]*,"* &c. in which he assigns a great superiority to the " Pontifex," while he sets the two powers on a par, *" because mankind is chiefly governed by these two offices* [p]*."*

Here we see how the example of Pope Gelasius, who had first used this style, was followed up in word and deed : not only was the Emperor excommunicated by a Papal Decree, but also it was now an established principle, that the Bishop of Rome, the " Pontifex," is *the spiritual sovereign of the world,* as the Emperor is *the temporal sovereign.*

[o] " Conferamus autem honorem imperatoris cum honore pontificis : inter quos tantum distat, quantum ille rerum humanarum curam gerit, iste divinarum."

[p] " Quia his præcipue duobus officiis regitur humanum genus." Mansi, viii. c. 215.

Some of the oriental Churches were in communion with Rome : these corresponded with Symmachus. There is a letter⁹ from them extant, asking for the Pope's protection, and submitting to his authority; and also a letter from the Pope to them. But who the parties were, does not appear. There were great dissensions at this time through parties in the Greek Church.

Under the name of Pope Symmachus, we find a letter containing the first recorded instance of a grant of the *pallium*, the consecrated scarf, which was the badge and certificate of Metropolitan authority from S. Peter : "*to shew that you are a Master and Archbishop, and that your Church shall be the Metropolitan See of the province of Pannonia ʳ;*" is the form of the letter addressed to Theodore, Archbishop of Laureacum (Lauriacum, Lorch on the Danube). Whether this letter

⁹ Mansi, viii. c. 218 and 221.

ʳ "Ad ostendendum te Magistrum et Archiepiscopum, tuamque ecclesiam provinciæ Pannoniorum sedem fore Metropolitanam." Symmach. Ep. xi. Mansi, c. 228.

be genuine or not, there can be little doubt that
the practice of bestowing the Pall was in use
about this time.   The letter speaks of it as a cus-
tomary thing [s].

The Pope's authority appears in another particular, which is indeed only an instance of what
was now usual.   The next Bishop of Arles, Cæ-
sarius [t], wrote to Symmachus, to restrain some
irregularities in his province of Arles : he says,
that as the Bishop's office is derived from S. Peter,
so the Pope must declare what is to be kept :
and then, after stating the points which needed
correction, he asks, "forbid all these things under
pain of your vengeance" ("hæc omnia ultione
districtionis vestræ fieri prohibete").   The Pope in
reply sent his edict, in the form of six Canons.
Thus the Pope's word was made law in the
provincial Churches by those Churches themselves : and the spiritual sovereignty which he
asserted was upheld by willing subjects.   This

[s] "Majorum more." Symmach. Ep. xi. Mansi, c. 228.
[t] Mansi, viii. c. 211, &c.

letter was written the year before the Pope's death [u].

Hormisdas succeeded Symmachus, A. D. 514, and sat for nine years. He engaged in the question between Rome and the Greek Church with activity. He corresponded with Anastasius the Emperor, and sent Legates to Constantinople, but could not gain his end. The Emperor, instead of being reconciled, was all the more incensed, and remained at variance until his death, A. D. 518.

Justin, who succeeded to the throne, was more favourable to peace, because he supported the Council of Chalcedon. But the Pope would admit no terms without the condemnation of Acacius, and the omission of his name in the Register of the Church : to which neither the Emperor nor the Church at Constantinople were willing to consent. At last, the Pope's perseverance prevailed; and on March 27, 519, John, the Patriarch of Constantinople, set his hand and signed his name to a confession of faith to the satis-

[u] Cos. Probo. Mansi, viii. c. 213. A. D. 513. Fast. Rom.

faction of the Pope, in which he condemned Acacius with Peter Mongus and other heretics[v].
Thus Rome and Constantinople were once more
in communion.

Before this settlement, the dispute had, during
the reign of Anastasius, run very high. Some
Churches had separated from the Greek communion, and joined Rome. This happened in Illyria
and the adjoining provinces[x]. John, the Bishop
of Nicopolis, the metropolis of Epirus, and the
Synod under him, sent in their adhesion to Rome:
and the Articles which Hormisdas sent in return
are worth noting.

John had sent the Pope a copy of the profession
which the Bishops of his province had adopted
in coming over to the Roman interest: the Pope
thinking he could improve on it, sent the following as more complete, which he bade him make
the Bishops subscribe to, thus[y]:—

"Regula Fidei. The first salvation is, to keep
the rule of the right faith, and not to devi-

v Mansi, viii. c. 451.   x Ibid. c. 411.

y Ibid. c. 407.

ate at all from the Constitutions of the Fathers. And because the words of our Lord Jesus Christ cannot be broken, when He said, *Thou art Peter, and on this rock I will build my Church*, &c. what was said was proved by the event, because religion has always been kept undefiled in the Apostolic Chair. Since therefore we wish not to be separated from this hope and faith, following in all things the Constitutions of the Fathers, we anathematize all heretics, especially Nestorius the heretic, who once was Bishop of Constantinople, and was condemned in the Council of Ephesus by Cælestinus Pope of Rome, and Saint Cyril Bishop of Alexandria. Together with him we anathematize Eutyches and Dioscorus of Alexandria, who were condemned in the holy Synod of Chalcedon, which we follow and adopt (*amplectimur*). To these we add Timothy the parricide, called Ælurus, and his pupil and follower Peter, or Acacius who remained in their company, because he deserved a sentence of condemnation like theirs, to whose communion he joined himself. Likewise we condemn Peter of Antioch, with his followers, and all the followers of the above-named persons.

"Therefore we receive and approve of all the Epistles of Pope Leo, which he wrote concerning the Christian religion. Whence, as we said before, following the Apostolic Chair in all things, and preaching all things which it ordains, I hope that I may deserve to be in one communion with you, which the Apostolic Chair preaches, in which is the entire and true solidity of the Christian religion. And I promise, as to those who are separated from the Communion of the Catholic Church z, that their names shall not be recited in the service (*mysteria*) of the Church.

"And this my profession I have subscribed with my own hand, and offered to thee, Hormisdas, holy and venerable Pope of Rome."

Dated, March 18, 517.

Such were the terms which Rome now herself prescribed for her own subjects. The Church

---

z " Sequestratos a communione ecclesiæ catholicæ, id est, non consentientes sedi Apostolicæ." Mansi, c. 408.

was literally, "addictus jurare in verba Magistri :" and communion with Rome, i. e. submission to the decrees of the Pope, was set forth *by Rome herself* as the foundation and substance of the religion of Christ.

Among the letters of Pope Hormisdas, of which eighty-one are preserved, there are some which are curious and peculiar, namely, his instructions to his Legates [a]. He used to give them written directions for their conduct, not only in transacting the business with which they were charged, but also for their deportment and conversation, putting words into their mouths, suggesting the probable answers which they might receive, and instructing them how to proceed farther on this or that supposition. These shew both the prudence and the ability of the Pope, and also the completeness and perfection now given to the system of policy, of which he was the head.

Hormisdas appointed Vicars Apostolic in several

---

[a] To Constantinople.   Mansi, viii. c. 389, 441.

Churches; as, Remigius [b], Bishop of Rheims in Gaul; in Spain [c], John, Bishop of Arragon; in Portugal [d], Sallustius.

The next Pope, John I, (A. D. 523) met with a different fate. The Emperor [e] Justin, being active against the Arians, excited the opposition of the Arian King Theodoric at Ravenna; who sent the Pope to Constantinople on a mission to Justin: on his return, Theodoric threw him into prison at Ravenna, where he died, A. D. 526 [f]. He was succeeded by Felix III.

Bonifacius II, who came next, had a rival, Dioscorus, elected at the same time, which caused a great schism: indeed, he seems to have been in a minority. He attempted after his rival's death to elect his own successor. But this being judged to be irregular, he was obliged formally to retract it; and he burnt publicly the deed of

[b] Mansi, viii. c. 383 and 525.
[c] Ibid. c. 429.
[d] Ibid. c. 433.
[e] Vita Joan. in Mansi, viii. c. 599.
[f] Olybrio Cons. Mansi, ibid.

conveyance, which he had executed. He died at the end of A. D. 532 [g].

Under him a Synod was held at Rome, in which the Archbishop of Larissa, and other Bishops from Thessaly, petitioned for protection against the Patriarch of Constantinople, who claimed authority over them. The case was examined; and the Supremacy of Rome was most fully acknowledged by the petitioners in their memorials. But, as the Manuscript in which the account was preserved is imperfect, the decision of the Council does not appear [h].

Under Pope John II, from A. D. 533 to A. D. 535, we find some peculiar points, which throw light on the state of the Roman Church. The Senate at Rome passed a law against Simony.

We have before this found the Senate acting with the Pope : the Senate took a prominent part in the dispute between Symmachus and Laurentius; and the Senate joined with Symmachus afterwards in excommunicating the Emperor

---

[g] Mansi, viii. c. 729. Anastas. Vit. Pont. i. p. 99.

[h] Mansi, c. 739, &c.

Anastasius. It seems that the removal of the royal residence from Rome to Ravenna, under the Gothic Kings, favoured the independent action of both Senate and Pope.

This *Senatus Consultum* had been made in Pope Bonifacius' II. time : and the young King Athalaric now confirmed it, with some additional regulations. It appears from the statements of the King's letter, that it was the practice for candidates for other Bishoprics also, as well as for the Papacy, to promise large sums of money to be paid after their appointment. It had happened, that a Bishop had been obliged to pawn (or sell) the Church plate, after he came into possession, in order to raise the money required to discharge what had been promised. These sums of money seem to have gone chiefly into the pockets of the officers of the Crown and the lawyers, who made their demands on the candidates before their appointments, and thus extorted large promises, perhaps took bonds for payment. It was also the custom for a Bishop to give away a considerable sum in "largess," distributed among the poor in his own (cathedral) town on his appointment.

The King now forbade all these simoniacal contracts before consecration, and ordered that the expenses of fees and law proceedings should be limited to 3000 solidi [i] (about £1870) for the election of the Pope, and 2000 solidi for any other Metropolitan Bishop, and that no Bishop should distribute to the people of his own town more than 500 solidi [j].

There is another letter from this same King Athalaric, on an important point concerning the Church. It is addressed to the Clergy of the Roman Church [k], and directs that suits against the Clergy (of which it alludes to some late cases) should be carried first into the Pope's Court. If justice was refused there, they should then be prosecuted in the Civil Courts. But if any one carried his suit into the Civil Court in contempt of the Pope's Court, he was to be fined

---

[i] According to Hoffman, from Gronovius.

[j] Mansi, viii. c. 891, &c.

[k] Cassiodor. Variar. viii. 24.

ten pounds of gold. This related to actions
about temporalities, not questions of doctrine.
And it shews, that criminal clerks had not yet
that exemption allowed them from all civil tribunals which they afterwards claimed: although
this law was a step towards such a conclusion.
The late King Theodoric had sent an order to
one of his judges to proceed against a priest
accused of robbing tombs, and to deprive him of
his ill-gotten gains, if found guilty[1]. Athalaric
expresses himself as if he granted the favour to
the Roman Church, because he could not shew
gratitude enough to God for raising him to the
throne. He concludes his letter with a word of
excellent advice to the Clergy, that they should
remember that their *"profession is a heavenly
life."*

The next Pope, Agapetus, who did not sit a
year, saw his authority triumph. The Emperor
Justinian sent him a letter of congratulation,
and submitted to him a confession of his faith[m],

---

[1] Cassiodor. Variæ. iv. 18.

[m] Mansi, viii. c. 845.

as was now becoming the custom; he was afterwards sent by the Gothic King Theodatus on a
mission to Constantinople, where he was received
with honour.

While there[n], he engaged in a dispute with the
Emperor concerning "The two Natures" of Christ:
and finding the Patriarch Anthimus to agree with
the Emperor, he accused him of heresy. The
Emperor was greatly offended, and threatened
him with banishment; but the Pope was firm:
the Emperor at last submitted, and the Patriarch was ultimately condemned, deposed, and
banished[o].

Agapetus also publicly condemned the irregular proceedings of Pope Boniface II. against
his rival Dioscorus the Anti-pope, and burnt the
subscriptions of the Clergy to an anathema (of
Dioscorus) which Boniface had extorted from the
Clergy[p].

Agapetus died at Constantinople, April 22, 536.

---

[n] Mansi, viii. c. 851, &c.
[o] Mansi, c. 869, 873, &c. Theophan. Anastas. p. 100, &c.
[p] Anastas. in Vit. Mansi, c. 841.

His successor Silverius was elected at Rome, under the influence of the Gothic King Theoda-tus[q], and his lot fell in troubled times. While Belisarius was besieged by the Goths under Viti-ges, he was accused of favouring the Goths, and thereupon banished by Belisarius[r]. He died soon afterwards, starved to death, it is reported, in his exile[s], A. D. 538.

Vigilius, who was elected next, came in upon the interest of the Court of Constantinople : he having, as it is said[t], given a promise to the Empress, that he would favour the Monophysite party. His career was not a glorious one in the annals of the Popedom : what he did, and what he suffered in connection with the Council of Constantinople, (fifth General) A. D. 553, appears in the history of that Council. In consequence of Vigilius' refusal to take part in the Council, the Council decreed[u], that his name should be

[q] Anastas. p. 102. Mansi, ix. c. 1.

[r] Evagrius, H. E. iv. 19. Marcellin. Chronic. in Gallandii Bibl. x. Victor Tunun. in Gallandii Bibl. xii.

[s] Liberat. Breviar. 22.

[t] Victor Tunun. Liberat. Breviar. 22.

[u] See the Acta in Mansi, ix. c. 345, &c.

erased and omitted from the diptychs, or registers
of the Church, in which it was the custom to
commemorate by name departed Bishops, but
without renouncing communion with the Church
of Rome.   This censure of the Pope, without sepa-
rating from the Church of Rome, is a distinct
denial of his Šupremacy.   The sentence of exclusion of the names of the Popes from the diptychs
remained in force from this time[x] at Constantinople.

We have now concluded a period of little more
than 200 years, since the doctrine of the Papal
Supremacy was first broached.   Look back for a
moment to survey the progress of it during these
two centuries, and you will perceive by what
means it increased: how gradually, insensibly,
and sometimes almost involuntarily, pretensions
grew up, and claims were enlarged; how these
were submitted to, and then acknowledged by
those upon whom they were made, until half the
world believed them to be just and right.   It
would be historically untrue to attribute all this

[x] Mich. Cerul. Epist. in Coteler. Monum. Eccl. Gr. v. ii. p. 140.

to the personal ambition of the Popes, of whom many, we cannot doubt, acted with good intentions, and were full of zeal for the name of Christ, and the welfare of His Church. Indisputably Rome often did good service to the Church: and every weakness in the separate members of the body, throughout the Roman empire, generally contributed to strengthen the ascendancy actually possessed by the leading See.

But yet, taking all these causes into the account, and making full allowance both for good motives in those who were most active, and for human infirmity in those who passively promoted it, the history of the growth of the Papal power, i. e. Popery, properly so called, exhibits clearly the rise and progress of a worldly principle within the Church.

Setting out from an acknowledged precedence among equals in rank, possessing from the first an actual influence well earned by distinguished merit, Rome proceeded by degrees to the fictions of S. Peter's supremacy, and the Pope's inheritance of a divine right to govern the whole Church.

When we observe how these doctrines, unheard
of in primitive ages, were first obscurely inti-
mated, then more broadly asserted, after this per-
petually referred to, introduced into every opening,
never omitted, but every incident taken advantage
of, and all circumstances dexterously turned into
an argument to support them; how succeeding
Popes never retracted, but adopted and uniformly
improved upon the pretensions of their predecessors; how an Innocent went beyond a Julius,
as Leo beyond Innocent, and a Gregory VII, in
later times, overshot him; when we see the care
and anxiety with which Popes seem in all things,
and sometimes above all things, to have provided
for the security of their own authority; and how
this end was carried out by interpolations and
falsification of ecclesiastical documents, which,
when detected, were never retracted or disavowed,
and somewhat later grew into a notorious and
scandalous system of forgery; when we weigh all
these things, it seems impossible for unprejudiced
readers to acquit the Papal Seat of the charge of
worldly ambition and corrupt motives.

Individual occupants differed in character; we must not suppose all were unprincipled: some were more, some less, free from human frailty; some were adorned by many virtues. But the system, founded on a false assumption, had this original error, that it was essentially a human polity: it was an ecclesiastical empire, which would maintain the Church of Christ by a power of the same kind as the secular, except that it claimed greater authority, and a more directly divine origin. And the corrupt seed which was mingled thus with the first plantation, did not fail to bring forth its proper fruit, from time to time, in the evident acts of personal ambition or unjustifiable arrogance of individual Popes, as well as the dishonest artifices of spurious documents and false authorities. The Church has since reaped a full harvest of bitterness, in her un-happy dissensions, for ages.

LECTURE III.

PART II.

The power of Rome seems to have made no further advance for some years after the middle of the sixth century. The Lombard wars, and the plague, depressed the energies of the Romans: and the See began to feel more sensibly the weight of Constantinopolitan influence when the conquests of Belisarius and Narses had brought Italy into subjection to the Emperor of the East again. The Patriarchs had never submitted to the Popes; from Vigilius' time they were in open feud with Rome; and now they had often the authority of the Emperor on their side against Rome. Vigilius was banished by Justinian. Pelagius I, who succeeded him, was opposed by the Romans, but supported by

Narses, Justinian's General [a].   And later the
Emperor Constans II, A. D. 666, sanctioned the
attempt of the See of Ravenna to make itself
independent of Rome [b].

The great and good Pope Gregory I, A. D.
590, in remonstrating against the Patriarch's
claim of the title, " Universal Bishop," has left
on record his own judgment against the Popes
of later ages, who in their pretensions and their
language went far beyond all that John of Constantinople claimed.   *" John, Bishop of Constantinople,"* he wrote, *" in opposition to God and the
peace of the Church, in contempt and to the injury
of all the Priesthood* (Bishops), *exceeded the bounds
of modesty and of his own measure, and unlawfully
took to himself in Synod the proud and pestilent
title of Ecumenic, that is, Universal (Bishop)* [c].*"*
Every word of this might be applied to the
Supremacy asserted by succeeding Popes.

[a] Anastas. p. 111.

[b] Muratori, Annal. 666.

[c] Gregor. Epist. ix. 68. See the point argued at length in
v. 18, 19, 20, 21. [And vii. 33 especially, which is omitted in
the Vatican MS.]

The disputes which arose in the East, in the seventh century, concerning the Nature of our blessed Lord [d], affected the West also. Several Patriarchs of Constantinople adopted the opinions of the Monothelites, and likewise one Pope, Honorius (A. D. 625) : in consequence of which, both the Pope and four Patriarchs were afterwards condemned by name [e] for that error, by the Council which assembled at Constantinople to judge of the Monothelite question, A. D. 680, called the Council in Trullus, or the sixth General Council.

Other Popes, however, had meanwhile condemned these same opinions : and one, Pope Martin, (A. D. 649) was cruelly persecuted, and suffered much violence from the Emperor Constans II, which ended in his banishment and death [f], because he resisted that Emperor's attempt to silence all further dispute on the question.

[d] The Monothelite controversy.

[e] See the Acta in Mansi, xi. c. 557, &c. c. 620.

[f] See the transactions in Mansi, x. c. 851, &c. and Galland. Biblioth. xiii. p. 43.

These events seem for a time to have humbled
the Papal spirit.   For, although Pope Theodore,
the predecessor of Martin, had been saluted by
the African Bishops in a fulsome style of more
than regal grandeur[g], as if in mockery of the
protests of Gregory I, Pope Agatho addressed
the Emperor at the Council in Trullus in the
following moving terms :

" Believe me in my low estate, most Christian
prince and son, that I pour forth these prayers
with tears for the stability and increase of your
power ; these things I am bold to advise out of
my sincere regard, although unworthy, and the
least of men ; because victory granted by God
to you is our safety, and your success is our joy.
Therefore with afflicted heart, and with tears
flowing inwardly in my mind, I fall down and
intreat you, deign to stretch out the right hand
of affection to the Apostolic doctrine, which the
blessed Apostle Peter, who aids your pious toils,

---

[g] Literally thus : "To the most blessed Lord, exalted to the
Apostolic height, the holy father of fathers, Theodore, Pope and
supreme Pontiff of all Bishops." (Domino beatissimo Apostolico
culmine sublimato sancto patri patrum, Theodoro, Papæ et
summo omnium Præsulum Pontifici.)   Mansi, x. c. 919.

has handed down[h]." The Popes of the eleventh and twelfth centuries addressed the Emperors in a tone different from this.

The Council of Constantinople, named Quinisextum, (sequel to the fifth and sixth General) which was called by the Emperor (Justinian Rhinotmetus), in A. D. 691, or 692, was adverse to the Supremacy of Rome; for it met independently of the Pope, and affirmed nothing of his authority, but made some Canons against Roman usages[i]. For which reason it was not at first received at Rome[j] by Pope Sergius. But John VII., the next Pope but one, accepted the Canons without alteration[k], A. D. 705. And the Council was also acknowledged again later by Pope Adrian I, A. D. 787[l], and by other Popes afterwards.

---

[h] Mansi, xi. c. 240. But Agatho did not omit to assert the Supremacy of S. Peter and his successors, after this humble appeal.

[i] Concerning the marriage of the Clergy, the Saturday's fast, and the rank of the Patriarch of Constantinople, &c. See the 102 Canons in Mansi, xi. c. 936.

[j] Anastas. Vit. Pontif. p. 150.

[k] Ibid. p. 157.   [l] Mansi, xii. c. 1079.

But while the independence of the Greek Church was becoming more and more hostile to the See of Rome, the Popes were beginning now to increase their influence in another way, by the acquisition of civil power and territory, and were preparing gradually to assume the character of a sovereign prince [m] among the powers of Europe, in addition to that of supreme sovereign of the whole Church.

Pope Gregory III. (A. D. 731) in the heat of the Iconoclastic controversy, had almost raised a civil war against the imperial government. He anathematized the Emperor Leo III. (Isaurian) and excited the Italians to renounce their allegiance to him [n]. Pope Stephen III. obtained from Pepin the possession of the Exarchate of Ravenna, as a donation to S. Peter [o]: which was confirmed and increased by a grant from Charle-

---

[m] See Koch, Tableau des Revol. i. p. 30.

[n] Theophanes Anastas. Vit. Pont. p. 174, &c.   Comp. Mansi, xii. c. 970, &c. where see two letters of P. Gregory II.

[o] In perpetuum pontificibus Apostolicæ Sedis possidendum, &c.   Anastas. Vit. Pont. p. 212.   And see Martene et Durand Veter. Script. Collectio ii. c. 1227.

magne to the next Pope Adrian I. A century afterwards, at the coronation of the Emperor Arnulfus, A. D. 896, we find the citizens of Rome inserting in their oath of allegiance [p] to the Emperor, a *salvo* of reservation for the allegiance due to the Pope (Formosus). But it was not until three centuries [q] later, after many political struggles between the Pope and the Romans, that Innocentius III. (A. D. 1198), the imperial throne being then vacant, exacted an oath of allegiance from the Prefect of Rome [r]. From that time the Prefect, senate, and magistrates, swore fealty to the Pope instead of the Emperor, and,

[p] Juro per hæc omnia Dei mysteria quod salvo honore et lege mea atque fidelitate Domini Formosi Papæ, fidelis sum et ero Arnulfo Imperatori, &c.   Muratori, Annali 896.

[q] Some reckon the independent sovereignty of the Popes in Rome to have begun from the time of Innocentius II, (A. D. 1130.) when the support of the Normans in Naples and Sicily enabled them to claim more civil power.   See L'Art de Verifier les Dates in Innocent II.

[r] Petrum Urbis Præfectum ad ligiam fidelitatem recepit, et per mantum quod illi donavit de Præfectura eum publice investivit, qui usque ad id tempus juramento fidelitatis imperatori fuerat obligatus et ab eo Præfecturæ tenebat honorem.   Gesta Innocent. III, p. 3. ed. Bosquet.

Muratori adds, "the authority of the Augusti breathed on that day its last gasp in Rome[s]." The same Pope secured to the See the possession of a great increase of territory, which had hitherto been often disputed; but was finally confirmed to the next Pope, Honorius III, and his successors, (A. D. 1220) by the Emperor Frederic II.[t]

The Council of Nicæa, A. D. 787, (named the seventh General) which condemned the Iconoclasts or figure-breakers, and authorized the use of figures[u] in Churches, although in it the Pope (Adrian I) complained[v] much of the Patriarch of Constantinople for calling himself Universal Bishop, must have tended on the whole to bring the two Churches more into union: for the Pope's Legates sat in the Council, and concurred in the decree which was made in favour of using figures.

[s] Spiro qui l' ultimo fiato l' autoritá degli Augusti in Roma. Annali, A. D. 1198. vii. p. 98.

[t] Mansi, xxii. c. 687. Muratori, Annal. 1198 and 1220. Martene et Durand. Vet. Script. Coll. ii. c. 1240.

[u] Not *images*, as it is sometimes popularly expressed: for the controversy was about *paintings* as much as *statues*.

[v] Mansi, xii. c. 1074.

But the result was not favourable to the Pope's Supremacy. For the Bishops of Charlemagne's dominions so little approved of this decree, that they met upon his summons at Frankfort-on-the-Maine, and in Council there condemned the worship of figures, and the second Council of Nicæa, A. D. 794.[x]

A statement which was made by Pope Adrian I at this Council illustrates the history of the Papacy, shewing what it was at that time. Adrian sent a long letter to the Council in defence of the use of figures, which letter contains the following story in support of his argument.

He says[y], when Constantine was first converted to Christianity, he saw one night a vision, in which S. Peter and S. Paul appeared to him, told him that Silvester, Bishop of Rome, was

---

[x] Pagi, A. D. 794. Mansi, xiii. c. 909, &c. For it seems that the "*Council of Constantinople*" named in the Canon must mean that of Nicæa, as Pagi explained it.

[y] Mansi, xii. c. 1057. [The story is given also with some other particulars by Moses Chorenens. ii. 80. p. 209, from Agathangelus.] 4to. Lond. 1736.

then lurking with some of his Clergy in Mount
Soracte to conceal himself from Constantine's
persecution, and bade him send ·for Silvester,
who should baptize him, and thus cure him of
the leprosy which then afflicted him. Constantine
accordingly sent for Silvester, found him as
described, and did all that he had been in the
vision bidden to do. He then asked, who *those
Gods*, Peter and Paul, might be. Silvester replied, they were not Gods, but the servants of
Christ. Constantine then asked, if there was any
figure of them preserved : and when the Pope
sent for paintings of the two Apostles, and shewed
them, the Emperor at once recognised them as
the persons who had appeared to him in the
vision. This was one of Pope Adrian's authorities
for the use of figures.

Concerning the history contained in this pre-
cious *morceau*, it is to be observed, that Silvester
was not Pope until the persecution was ended;
that Constantine never persecuted in Italy, his
coming into Italy put a stop to the persecution;
that he was not baptized by Silvester, nor bap-

tized at all until his last illness, and then at Nico-
media, most probably by Eusebius; that there
is no notice in history of his ever having been
afflicted by leprosy, and it is most incredible that
he ever was.   The infallibility of Pope Adrian,
which *ought* to be the voucher for this story,
involves here the *veracity* of the two Apostles,
who are both made to assert in the vision what
was untrue.   What then can we think of the
judgment of an " Infallible Head" which could be
imposed upon by such paltry stuff for history,
or of the *honesty* of a man who could wilfully
attempt to impose upon the world and the Church
by such gross falsehoods?   But by such aids the
Supremacy grew up.

> Sic fortis Etruria crevit,
> Scilicet et rerum facta est *pulcherrima Roma.*

This was asserted gravely and authoritatively,
and sent with all solemnity to what was intended
to be a General Council of the Church.   As the
narrative was taken, doubtless, from some spurious "Memorials," it shews what kind of books
now passed current at Rome for "Papal His-

M

tories." Did the Popes *know* what these were really worth, or *did they not?* The answer either way is fatal to the credit of "*S. Peter's Chair.*"

The great dispute concerning Photius, and his right to the Patriarchate, in the ninth century, which led to the final separation between Rome and Constantinople, strengthened the authority of the former over the minds of men by the victory which it gained: while the moral force of the testimony which the Church of Constantinople has left on record against the false pretensions and tyranny of the Pope, is weakened by the manifest defects of their case[y], and some want of temperance in the mode of conducting it. But here, as usual, Rome grew strong through the weaknesses of other Churches[z]. Ignatius triumphed over his opponent Photius in the Council at Constantinople, A. D. 869. (named the eighth General) by means of Rome: and

[y] For the deposition of Ignatius, although allowed by Rome at first, seems to have been irregular in the first instance.

[z] [Under P. Nicolas I. (A. D. 858–867) there was a great increase in the practice of referring questions to Rome for advice or decision. Anastas. V. P. p. 602.]

therefore naturally acknowledged the authority to
which he was so much indebted; and the Popes,
Nicolas I, who died a little before that Council
met, and Adrian II, his successor, did not lose the
opportunity which the Council gave, of asserting
their pretensions in the fullest terms.   Nicolas
laid it down, that *no question could be decided
without the consent of the Roman pontiff* [a] : that
*Rome is the rule of faith, and the source of ab-
solution* [b].   The judgment of Rome he calls *the
voice of God* [c].   Ignatius acknowledged him to be
the successor of the prince of the Apostles, the
chief shepherd, and divine pontiff [d].   The Roman
Church saluted Adrian with the title, *Coangelical
Lord Pope* [e].   His Legates in the Council steadily
affirmed, that "they did not come to the Council
for the case to be tried : but that it had already

[a] Mansi, xvi. c. 59; comp. 126.

[b] Ibid. c. 69.

[c] Quoniam audisti vocem Dei per Apostolicæ Sedis officium
tibi delatam, &c. he writes to the Emperor Basilius.   Ibid.
c. 120.

[d] Ibid. c. 47.

[e] Domine coangelice Papa.   Ibid. c. 28, 124.

been tried and decided at Rome, there was no room for enquiry or judgment: the Council had met for nothing but to hear the judgment of Rome, &c[1]."

Thus we see how the jurisdiction of Rome had increased; from receiving appeals, which was all that the Sardican Canon gave, to the revising all judgments *ex officio,* and now to the claiming to be *the supreme executive,* by whose authority alone any judgment in the Church could be valid.

Rome having advanced so far against Constantinople, while her power was constantly on the increase throughout the West, Pope Leo IX. found no difficulty in bringing the dispute to a summary conclusion, when it was renewed two centuries afterwards, by a sentence of excommunication upon Michael Cerularius the Patriarch, A. D. 1054. This was not a synodical judgment, but a Papal decree, an anathema pronounced in the Pope's name, upon the Primate of the Eastern Church and all his followers. It

[1] Mansi, c. 56.

began thus : " Humbert, by the grace of God Cardinal Bishop of the Roman Church, Peter Archbishop of Amalfi, Frederic Deacon and Chancellor, to all the sons of the Catholic Church. The holy Roman Chief and Apostolic Chair, to which as head belongs specially the care of all the Churches, for the sake of the peace and good of the Church has deigned to send us her Commissioners (Apocrisarios) to this royal city, that, as it is written[g], we *might go down and see whether they have done altogether according to the cry of it, which is come unto me ; and if not,* he *might know.* Wherefore let the glorious Emperor know," &c.. Then follows a statement of the charges against the Patriarch ; after which the edict continues, " For which errors and many other deeds, this Michael being admonished by the letters of our Lord Pope Leo refused to repent," &c. — " Wherefore, we not bearing the unheard-of insult and wrong of the

[g] Genes. xviii. 21. The Pope here applies to his Legates the language of the Almighty. The wording of the passage quoted is not quite the same as in the Vulgate.

Chief and Apostolic Chair, and perceiving that
the Catholic faith is in many ways assailed, by
authority of the holy and undivided Trinity, and
of the Apostolic Chair, whose Legates we are,
and of all the orthodox Fathers of the Seven
Councils, and of the whole Catholic Church,
thus subscribe to the anathema, which our Lord
the most Reverend Pope has denounced upon
the aforesaid Michael and his followers, unless
they would repent [h]."

According to this precedent, the Pope had
authority to *pronounce an anathema by commission*
upon whatever portion of the Church he pleased.
Such was the doctrine of the Supremacy in the
eleventh century.

If Pope Julius, who certainly did not want
either courage or a due sense of the dignity of
his See, had but known that he possessed by
divine right this power as successor to S. Peter,
how gladly would he have employed it in defence
of the Nicene Faith, against the Arian Patriarch
of Constantinople in the fourth century!

[h] The sentence is in Mansi, xix. c. 678.

Truly the successors of S. Peter in early ages were as ignorant of the powers bequeathed to them, as the holy Apostle wás of all command to convey such plenary authority. It was reserved for the Popes of the eleventh and the following two centuries fully to " *develope*" the mind of our Lord and of His Apostle, concerning the rights of the vicarious head of the Church.

But the Papal triumph over the Greek Church was not complete, until, after that the first crusade had conquered Constantinople, when the Patriarch Germanus wrote to Pope Gregory IX. protesting that the Greeks were not schismatics, and entreating him to be at peace with them, that Pope, A.D. 1232, could exult over the downfall of the Greek Church, which was now " *reduced to obedience under Rome* [i]," and taunt the Patriarch with the arrogant boast, that "*calamities had come by the just judgment of God* [j], *ever since they had refused*

---

[i] See Gregory the Ninth's Letter to King Louis, in Mansi, xxiii. c. 107.

[j] Cum Græcorum ecclesia a Romanæ sedis unitate recessit, statim privilegio caruit ecclesiasticæ libertatis : et quæ libera

obedience to S. Peter and his successors; while the Roman Church, the '*head and mistress of all Churches,*' had flourished in peace."

When the Western Church was finally separated from the Eastern, especially as the latter was also now miserably reduced and weakened by the conquests of the Saracens, the West, which had before been accustomed to domineer in deportment toward the East, was now all the more disposed to fall into the error of considering itself to be the *whole* Church : and the Pope, as

fuerat, facta est sæcularis potestatis ancilla, ut justo Dei judicio, quæ noluit Divinum recognoscere in Petro primatum, toleret invita dominium sæculare, &c. Mansi, xxiii. c. 58. The Emperor Alexius actually had written to Pope Innocentius III. asking him to make the *reduction of the Greek Church to obedience to the Apostolic Chair one object of the crusade.* Pope Innocentius did not exactly assent to Alexius' request at that time. He only threatened the Patriarch with what he *might* do, "*si in Græcorum ecclesias procedere compellamur.*" (p. 41.) But at all events it is clear, from Alexius' request, that this abominable pretext of invading and conquering the Greek Church *on a religious principle,* by a crusade, had been discussed and put forward in high quarters, and communicated to the Pope, who does not appear to have objected to it, even if he did not allow it nor act upon it. See Gesta Innocent. III, p. 39.

the Chief of the West, seemed naturally, as it were, to fill the place of Chief of the whole Church. Councils, which heretofore had been composed of representatives from both divisions of Christendom, were now called from the West alone; and instead of being *Œcumenical*, or, of the whole Church, which only made a really *General* Council, such as those which had authority in earlier ages, they were now *Roman* Councils[j] : summoned no longer by the Emperors from all parts of Christendom : but by the Popes, from those parts which were entirely subject to their authority, to meet at Rome, or wherever

[j] In some Collections of Councils a distinction is made between *Œcumenical* and *General*. The earlier Councils, called from the whole Church, are named *Œcumenical*, those called from the Western Church only are named *General*. See Mansi, and Baluzius. Bellarmine makes no such distinction; but regards the Councils (of which he reckons the whole number to be eighteen) both before and after the separation of the East from the West, as *General* alike, De Controvers. vol. ii. De Conc. i. 5. ed. Par. 1608. P. Sarpi says, that after the separation the Greeks called *that* a general Council in which the five Patriarchs met, the Latins *that* where the Western Church met under the Pope. Conc. de Trente, 1. 2. p. 9, 10. ed. Courayer. Amst. 1736.

else the Pope might fix his seat. The eighth
General Council had been called by the Emperor
Basilius, at the request of Pope Adrian, A.D. 869 [k].
The third Lateran Council was called by Pope [l]
Alexander III, A. D. 1179, in the same manner as
it had been formerly done by the Emperors [m].

Another change in the Councils was, that
although they assembled as if General, the Decrees or Canons were not now as in former times
the judgment and joint act of the Council, but
Constitutiones, or *Decretals*, *of the Pope, promulgated
by the Pope* to the Council, sometimes said to be

[k] Mansi, xvi. c. 22.

[l] A considerable step towards this conclusion was made by the
seventeenth Canon of that eighth Council, which decreed, that
the five Patriarchs have power over their own Metropolitans,
and can summon them to Council ; which summons, the Metropolitans are bound to obey, even against the will of their secular
Princes. Mansi, xvi. c. 157. Sess. 10. [The letter of the Emperor Constantine, read at the seventh Council, stated the law
otherwise. Mansi, xii. c. 1003.]

[m] See the form of the summons in Mansi, xxii. c. 211, referred
to as "Ad omnes Episcopos," in xxi. c. 909. But the practice
began earlier, although apparently with less ostentation at first.
For Pope Callistus II, writing to the Emperor Henry V, says,
that the first Lateran Council, A. D. 1123, had been appointed
by him, *Concilium indictum a nobis accelerat.* Mansi, xxi. c. 281.

approved by the Council [n]. Indeed they derived their force, according to the maxims of these times, not from the Council, but from the Pope. For Gregory VII, in a Council at Rome A. D. 1074, laid down the law, that the first four General Councils, which he compares to the four Gospels, ought to be highly reverenced indeed, but not so highly as the decrees of the Roman Pontiffs, since *those very Councils would have no force, unless the Pontiffs of the Apostolic Chair had decreed that the same should be collected and confirmed by* (their) *Apostolic authority* [o]. This was a doctrine different from that of the fourth General

---

[n] The first Canon of the first Lateran Council was in the name of the Pope: *Officii nostri* debita innovantes ordinari—*auctoritate sedis Apostolicæ prohibemus*, &c. Mansi, xxi. c. 282. And in the Canonization of Conrad: in generali quod celebramus Concilio—nunciamus—constituimus, &c. ibid. c. 289. The seventh Can. of the second Lateran runs thus, " *We following the steps of our predecessors, Gregory VII. Urban, and Paschal,*" &c. The *We*, in whose names the Council spoke, therefore, is *the Pope*. Mansi, xxi. c. 527. Approbante Concilio, in the third Lateran, Mansi, xxii. c. 217. Innocent III. himself says, he will decide *auctoritate sedis Apostolicæ, ac sacri approbatione Concilii*. Gesta Innocent. p. 41.

[o] Mansi, xx. c. 405.

Council of Chalcedon, A. D. 451, in which the letter of Pope Leo was read, and then examined to see whether it was orthodox, according to the Nicene Faith; and each member of the Council was asked to give his opinion on this question, before the letter was received p.

When the Popes had become absolute over Councils, they made laws for their own election. Nicolas II, A. D. 1058, in a Council at Rome, published a " *Decree* q," that thenceforth the *Cardinals alone should choose the Pope :* which made the dignity of Cardinal much more in request from that time. He also made the ordinance, " that a preference should be given to Romans in the election."

Of the other new claims of authority which were gradually evolved from the doctrine of the Supremacy, it is to be observed, that *the right to dispose of temporal sovereignties* was assumed by

---

p See the fourth Session. Mansi, vii. c. 9.

q The Cardinal (7) Bishops were first to debate, then to call in the Cardinal Clergy, and then the other Clergy and people were to assent to the election. Pagi, A. D. 1059. iv.

Nicolas II, A. D. 1059, when he took upon him-self to confirm the Duke of Calabria and Sicily in the possession of his dominions, on certain con-ditions[r], for which dominions the Duke swore fealty to the Pope[s]; and again by the next Pope Alexander II. when he gave his sanction to William the Norman's invasion of England[t]. Alexander III. gave Henry II. a grant of the possession of Ireland[u]: and Innocentius IV. like-wise bestowed the kingdom of Portugal on the Count de Bologna[x], A. D. 1245.

The power which could confer, could also take away. And accordingly the next step of advance in this direction was, that the Popes should claim authority to *depose princes from their thrones:* as Gregory VII, A. D. 1076, did to the Em-peror Henry IV, releasing his subjects from their allegiance, and urging the Princes of Germany

r Pagi, A. D. 1059. xii.

s See the Forms used to Pope Gregory VII. Mansi, xx. c. 313.

t Matth. Paris, p. 2. ed. Lond. 1684.

u Hoveden, ed. Savile, Franc. 1601, p. 528. Brompton, in Twysden Script. x. p. 1069.

x At the first Council of Lyons. Mansi, xxiii. c. 652.

to elect a new Emperor [y], which sentence was [z] continued by succeeding Popes; Alexander III. to the Emperor Frederic I, A. D. 1168 [a]; Inno-

---

[y] This memorable sentence is worth quoting from. It is in the form of a prayer, beginning thus: BLESSED PETER, PRINCE OF THE APOSTLES, INCLINE THINE EAR TO US, WE BESEECH THEE, AND HEAR ME THY SERVANT, &c.—THOU ART MY WITNESS, AND MY LADY THE MOTHER OF GOD, AND S. PAUL THY BROTHER, AND ALL THE SAINTS, THAT THE ROMAN CHURCH BROUGHT ME AGAINST MY WILL TO THY GOVERN-MENT—AND THEREFORE OF THY GRACE, AND NOT OF MY OWN GOOD WORKS, I BELIEVE IT IS, THAT IT HATH PLEASED THEE AND DOTH PLEASE THEE, THAT THE PEOPLE OF CHRIST SPECIALLY EN-TRUSTED TO THEE SHOULD OBEY ME IN YOUR STEAD, AND BY YOUR GRACE POWER IS GIVEN TO ME BY GOD TO BIND AND LOOSE IN HEAVEN AND EARTH. THEREFORE, RELYING ON THIS TRUST FOR THE HONOUR AND DEFENCE OF THY CHURCH, IN BEHALF OF ALMIGHTY GOD THE FATHER, AND THE SON, AND THE HOLY GHOST, I DENY TO HENRY THE GOVERNMENT OF THE WHOLE REALM OF GERMANY AND ITALY, AND RELEASE ALL CHRISTIANS FROM THE BOND OF THE OATH WHICH THEY HAVE MADE OR WILL MAKE TO HIM, AND FORBID ANY ONE TO SERVE HIM AS IF HE WERE A KING, &c.   Mansi, xx. c. 467.

[z] Mansi, xxi. c. 277.

[a] Ibid. xxii. c. 34.

cent III. to the Emperor [b] Otto IV, A. D. 1210, and to King John, A. D. 1212 [c]; Gregory IX, A. D. 1238 [d], and Innocent IV, A. D. 1245 to the Emperor Frederic II [e]; John XXII. to Ludovic King of Bavaria, A. D. 1333 [f], and Pius V. to Queen Elizabeth, A. D. 1569 [g].

Another case exhibits the assumption of the twofold power of giving and taking away dominions in one and the same act. When the crusade against the Albigenses, A. D. 1208, which the third Lateran Council, A. D. 1179, had before authorized [h], had effected the conquest of Toulouse and the adjoining countries

b Trithem. Chron. i. ed. S. Gall. 1690. p. 517. Mansi, xxii. c. 813.   c Matth. Paris, p. 195.

d Mansi, xxiii. c. 78. Trithem. Chron. i. p. 570.

e Mansi, xxiii. c. 613. Matth. Paris, p. 589.

f Trithem. Chron. ii. p. 159. The Popes excommunicated several Princes beside these. Innocentius III, A. D. 1210, excommunicated a King of Armenia. See Epist. ii. 64, 66. ed. 1635.

g Collier, Eccl. Hist. ii. p. 521.

h Canon 27. De Hereticis. Mansi, xxii. c. 232. This Canon condemns the Albigenses and many other heretics, proscribes them from all intercourse, and exhorts all people to take up arms against them, promising pardon of sins to all who died truly penitent in that cause, &c.

from the Count of Toulouse, it was a question, what should be done with the conquered territory. The Pope's Legates for a while held provisional possession of the country [i] : until the Pope, Innocentius III, directed a Bull to Simon, Count de Montfort, conferring the dominion of the territory upon him, and declaring the Count of Toulouse deprived of all right to it [j]. Bonifacius [k] VIII. (VII.) wrote to King Edward I, that the kingdom of Scotland was the special property of the Roman Church, and therefore he must not touch it. Innocentius III. declared [l], that God had ordained the Pope as Christ's Vicar, to have power over all *nations*

[i] Mansi, xxii. c. 938.

[j] Mansi, c. 935. It was confirmed again in the fourth Laterān Council, A. D. 1215. Mansi, c. 1069.

[k] Mansi, xxiv. c. 1136, &c.

[l] Summum Apostolicæ Sedis et Romanæ. ecclesiæ pontificem, quem in b. Petro sibi vicarium ordinavit, super gentes et regna constituit, evellendi, destruendi, disperdendi, et dissipandi, et ædificandi et plantandi ei conferens potestatem, loquens ad eum in Propheta, &c. Bullar. Roman. Cherubini, i. p. 37. This was to the King of Bulgaria : and he repeated it to King John, A. D. 1215. See Matth. Paris, p. 224.

and kingdoms, to root out, and to pull down, and to destroy, and to throw down, and to build, and to plant, applying to the Papacy the words of God spoken to the Prophet Jeremiah[m].

The next Pope Bonifacius VIII. adopted these principles, and improved upon them. Besides a Decree, by which he bestowed Sardinia and Corsica upon James King of Aragon, under condition of a yearly payment of 2000 marks to the Apostolic Chair, which begins with these words[n], *"Being set above kings and kingdoms by a divine preeminence of power, we dispose of them as we think fit,"* &c. (A. D. 1303) he published in the famous Bull called "Unam Sanctam," A. D. 1302, a statement of the authority which he claimed, so full and complete, that it may stand for the authorized exposition of the doctrine of the Supremacy. It contains the following propositions, which are literally translated, the intervening and less important part being omitted.

[m] Jer. i. 10,

[n] Bullarium Romanum Cocquelines, iii. pt. 2. p. 82.

N

We are bound by the obligation of the faith to believe and hold, that there is one holy Catholic and Apostolic Church. — Therefore of this one and only Church there is one Body and one Head,—namely, Christ, *and Christ's Vicar, Peter, and his successor.—Therefore if either the Greeks, or any other, say that they are not entrusted to Peter, they must confess that they are not Christ's flock.*—And we are taught by the words of the Gospel, that there are in *this his* (Peter's) *power two swords, the spiritual and the temporal :— each therefore (of these) is in the power of the Church.—But one sword ought to be inferior to the other sword, and the temporal authority to be subject to the spiritual power.* — For according to S. Dionysius, (*the forged works in the name of Dionysius the Areopagite*) the divine law is, &c. — For as, the truth witnesses, *the spiritual power. has to institute, and to judge the earthly power, if it be evil: thus the prophecy of Jeremiah proves concerning the Church and the power of the Church,* See, I have this day set thee, &c. (as above). — Therefore *if the earthly power err, it will be judged by the spiritual power.   But if the spiritual power err, the inferior will be judged by his superior.   But if the highest (spiritual power) err, no man, but God alone, will have power to judge it.*   Since the Apostle witnesses, He that is spiritual judgeth all things: yet he himself is judged of no man.   But this authority, which is *not human but rather divine, is given by the Divine lips to Peter, and confirmed to him and his successors.*— Therefore whoever resists this power so ordained by God, *resists the ordinance of God, unless, like a Manichæan, he pretend that there are two First Principles:* which we declare to be false and heretical. — Moreover WE DECLARE, AFFIRM, DEFINE, AND PRONOUNCE, THAT IT IS ALTOGETHER NECESSARY FOR SALVATION, THAT EVERY HUMAN CREATURE SHOULD BE SUBJECT TO THE ROMAN PONTIFF [o].

[o] Unam sanctam Ecclesiam Catholicam et ipsam Apostolicam urgente fide credere cogimur et tenere.—Igitur Ecclesiæ unius et unicæ unum Corpus, unum Caput.—Christus videlicet et Christi Vicarius Petrus, Petrique Successor.—Sive ergo Græci, sive alii, se dicant Petro non esse commissos, fateantur necesse se de ovibus Christi non esse.—In hac ejusque potestate duos esse gladios, spiritualem videlicet et temporalem, Evangelicis dictis instruimur.—Uterque ergo est in potestate Ecclesiæ.—

The contest between the Pope and Philip the Fair, King of France, against whom this was directed, and upon whom the Pope also passed a sentence of Excommunication and Deposition P, was so hot, that it came at last to personal violence; and the Pope is generally believed to have died of chagrin, a few weeks after he had

Oportet autem gladium esse sub gladio, et temporalem auctori‑tatem spirituali subjici potestati.— Nam secundum beatum Dionysium, lex divinitatis est, infima per media in suprema reduci.— Nam veritate testante, spiritualis potestas terrenam potestatem instituere habet et judicare, si bona non fuerit: sic de ecclesia et ecclesiastica potestate verificatur vaticinium Hiere‑miæ, Ecce constitui te.—Ergo, si deviat terrena potestas judi‑cabitur a potestate spirituali.   Sed si deviat spiritualis, minor a suo superiori; si vero suprema, a solo Deo, non ab homine pot‑erit judicari : testante Apostolo, Spiritualis homo judicat omnia, ipse autem a nemine judicatur.   Est autem hæc auctoritas—non humana, sed potius divina, ore divino Petro data, sibique suis‑que successoribus—firmata—.   Quicunque igitur huic potestati a Deo sic ordinatæ resistit, Dei ordinationi resistit; nisi duo, sicut Manichæus, fingat esse principia : quod falsum et hæreti‑cum judicamus.—Porro subesse Romano Pontifici omnem huma‑nam creaturam declaramus, dicimus, definimus, et pronuntiamus omnino esse de necessitate salutis.   Datum Lateran. Pontificat. nostri. a. viiiº.   See Sextus Lib. Decretal. Extravagant. i. p. 219. and the Acta inter Bonifacium. &c. et Philippum Pulchrum, printed in 1614. p. 12.

P Bullarium Roman. Cocquelines, vol. iii. pt. 2. p. 103.

been rescued from William de Nogaret the French King's Officer, who had seized him at Anagni.

The opposition from France made the next Pope but one, Clemens V, judge it expedient to concede something : and accordingly he published a Bull, by which he revoked the Bull " Unam Sanctam," so far, that France should be in *no greater degree* subjected to the Roman Church than *it had been before :* he also decreed the same with regard to another Bull of Pope Bonifacius, " Clericis Laicos :" but in this it was only intended to relieve the kingdom of France [q] : there was no renunciation of the principles asserted by Bonifacius, nor condemnation of his claims as false and unfounded.   And the Bull, "Unam Sanctam," stands printed with a large commentary on it in the Decretalia [r].   So that we have a right still to consider it an authentic declaration of the real nature of the claims of the Supremacy [s].

[q] See the Acta inter Bonifac. &c. et Philipp. p. 101.

[r] See the Sextus Liber, as above.   Paris, 1561.

[s] [It was adopted and confirmed by Leo X. in his Bull, which revoked the Pragmatic Sanction, and gave the Concordat to France.   Fleury xxv. p. 440, A. D. 1516.] ed. Par. 1751.

The Crusades brought out a new feature of the Papal power, not only by the extension of influence which they gave to the Popes, but also by a doctrinal "development," that of *pardons or indulgences.*

Urban II, at the Council of Clermont 1095, held out the hope of pardon for sin, as an inducement to take the Cross, promising this on S. Peter's authority[t]: "*We, trusting in the mercy of God, and the authority of S. Peter and S. Paul,* to all faithful Christians who take up arms, &c.—*relax infinite penances for their misdeeds.* But let those who shall die there in true repentance, not doubt that *they will have pardon of their sins and the fruit of eternal reward.* Meanwhile we take under shelter of the Church and the protection of S. Peter and S. Paul, all those who with ardent faith undertake the labour of conquering the infidels," &c.

A similar promise was made in the first Lateran Council, A. D. 1123, to the crusaders against the

---

[t] Mansi, xx. c. 823.

infidels[u], and in the third Lateran Council to the crusaders against the Albigenses heretics[x]. And Innocentius III, in the fourth Lateran, A. D. 1215, according to the law of the Papal "development," went beyond his predecessors in the amplitude of his offers to either crusade[y]. *"We therefore, trusting in the mercy of Almighty God, and the authority of the blessed Apostles Peter and Paul, and that power of binding and loosing which God has given us, however unworthy of it, to all those who undergo this labour in person, or by furnishing the cost of it, grant* (indulgemus) *a full pardon of their sins, which they shall with real contrition have confessed, and in the recompense of the just we promise them an increase of eternal salvation[z]."*

But the same Pope Innocentius III. surpassed even this, by the terms in which he asserted the

---

u At Jerusalem or in Spain, Can. xi. Mansi, xxi. c. 284.

x Mansi, xxii. c. 232.

y Ibid. c. 987. in Canon iii. Catholici vero, &c.

z Ibid. c. 1067. Gregory IX. repeated this form in his Epistle 8, to the English, A. D. 1235. Mansi, xxiii. c. 70.

power of the Pope to forgive sins. It is an awful
sentence to come from the pen of a Christian
Bishop: I will give it in his own words.

Speaking of the saying of our Lord, that a
brother should be forgiven *"seventy times seven
times,"* he writes, to the Patriarch of Constantinople [a]: *"the number seven multiplied into itself in
this place signifies all the whole sins of all men, all
which Peter alone can remit, and not only these,
but also the accusations of all men* [acquit of all
charges?]—*The Lord suffered Peter alone to be
his Vicegerent in office, and his successor in power.
Therefore after the Lord's ascension, Peter began
to govern the Church as His successor.—Who when
he had consecrated the Roman Church by his own
blood, bequeathed the primacy of the Chair to his*

[a] Septenarius ergo numerus in seipsum multiplicatus, in hoc
loco significat universorum universa peccata, quæ solus Petrus
potest non solum omnia, sed omnium crimina relaxare—solum
Petrum sustinuit sibi Dominus, et in officio Vicarium, et in
magisterio successorem. Unde post ascensionem Domini Petrus
velut successor ipsius regere cœpit Ecclesiam—Qui cum Romanam ecclesiam suo sanguine consecrasset, primatum Cathedræ
successori reliquit, totum in eo transferens plenitudinem potestatis, &c. Gesta Innocent. III. p. 43.

*successor, transferring to him the whole plenitude
of power.*" The POPE ALONE in the PLENITUDE
of his POWER could REMIT ALL SINS of ALL MEN !
So said a Pope of his own office. And he is
supposed by virtue of his office to be infallible.

There can be little doubt how such *promises*,
backed by such assertions of authority, would
have been understood by *the people* in those ages.
And the transition from this to the extreme abuse
of "indulgences" was easy, for the practice was
ever on the increase. Pope Bonifacius VIII,
A. D. 1300 [b], instituted the jubilees, and granted
larger indulgences to all who should visit the
Church of S. Peter and S. Paul, at the end of
each century. " In the *plenitude of Apostolic
power,*" are his words, " *we will grant, and do
grant,* not only full and larger, *but even the fullest
pardon of all their* sins." P. Clemens VI. increased
the favour, and granted the same indulgence for
a jubilee on the fiftieth year, Æ. D. 1350 [c].

b Trithem. Chron. ii. p. 78. " Non solum plenam et largiorem,
imo plenissimam omnium suorum concedemus et concedimus,
veniam peccatorum." Bullar. Rom. Cocquelines, iii. part. 2. p. 94.
Cherubini, i. p. 145.   c Trithem. Chron. ii. p. 213.

Another display of the Supremacy ought not to be omitted. In the fourth Lateran Council, A. D. 1215, it was decreed, " *by Innocentius III, with the approval of the* Council[d]," that *all Princes* should *purge their dominions of all heretics, and exterminate them to the utmost of their power,* or else *they should be deposed by the Pope, and their dominions given to* " Catholics [e]."

This decree, besides the authority which it assumed over all temporal powers, placed the lives and liberties of all subjects in the hands of papal agents and papal courts, upon every suspicion of unsound doctrine ; and made the *Supremacy responsible* for the *guilt of the cruelty or injustice* which *might* follow : for it all *emanated from* that one *universal authority.*

The Inquisition, which soon afterwards arose upon this principle, was a natural sequel to such a decree, and was likewise *the act of the Supremacy.*

---

d That Pope's own words, see p. 171, note n.

e Can. 3. De Hæreticis, Mansi, xxii. c. 987. The passage, literally translated, has been already quoted in a note at the end of the Preface.

The advance of the Papal Supremacy on the liberties of the Clergy is remarkable. It gradually encroached on their ecclesiastical discipline, property, ministrations, and spiritual office, until it had left them neither authority nor function, except what was derived from S. Peter's Chair.

We have seen how from the appellate jurisdiction, first given by the Canons of Sardica in 347, the Supremacy had increased, until Pope Nicolas asserted (867), that no question in the Church could be decided without the consent of the Roman Pontiff, and Gregory VII. that Councils and Canons derive their force from the authority of Rome.

Thither, accordingly, every ecclesiastical cause was to be carried for final determination. The burden of constant appeals to Rome was one of the grievances .cried out against, throughout Europe, and in England especially, for centuries.

Legates, Vicars Apostolic, or decrees from Rome, claimed implicit obedience from all the Clergy.

Exemptions from episcopal control were given by Popes to religious houses at their pleasure: and the Monasteries were often the favoured supporters of the Papal authority against the Bishops or the national Churches.

The English Archbishops were required to go [f] to Rome to receive the Pallium from the Pope, which alone conferred Metropolitan authority; for this they had to pay immense sums in the shape of fees at Rome, beside the expense incurred by tolls levied in the countries through which they passed on their journey [g].

The property of the Church was claimed entirely by the Popes of the middle ages.

Innocentius II. asserted this authority at the second Lateran Council, (1139) in the following

[f] Dunstan went to receive the Pall, A. D. 961. See Osbern in Angl. Sacr. ii. p. 109. Gervas. Act. Pontif. in Twysden Script. x. p. 1646. Lanfranc asked to have it sent to him from Pope Alexander II. It was refused him until he went for it. See Archdeacon Hildebrand's Letter to Lanfranc. Epist. vi. p. 222. of Lanfranc. Oper. ed. 1745.

[g] See Canute's complaint to Pope John XIX. A. D. 1031, in Wilkins' Concil. i. p. 297.

terms: "You know that Rome is the head of the world, and that *the dignity of ecclesiastical honour is received by the license of the Roman Pontiff, by the custom of a kind of feudal right, and it is not held legally without his permission* [h]."

And it was no empty boast, but was acted upon without reserve. The Popes by their Legates and otherwise, beside subsidies of money raised for the use of Rome, usurped the patronage of the Church, and bestowed the benefices on their own favourites, and these often foreigners and non-resident, while the national Clergy were starving [i]. Such was the complaint made in the first Council of Lyons, A. D. 1245, by the Proctors of the Peers and Commons of England, to which Pope Innocentius IV. listened in gloomy silence [k].

[h] Chronic. Mauriniacense in Mansi, xxi. c. 534.

[i] It is not to my present purpose, and it would be tedious, to recite all that was said in complaint against the rapacity and injustice of the papal agents and papal courts, in exacting money, from Matthew of Paris, Eadmer, Petrus Blesensis, and others.

[k] Matth. Paris, p. 585. The Brevis Nota in Mansi, xxiii. c. 612. passes very briefly over the subject.

And the Canon which was afterwards passed in that same Council on the subject, to the effect, that Legates *have no power to give away Benefices, unless specially commissioned to do so*[1], while it seemed to promise little practical relief of the grievance, was really an insult to the complainers, by reaffirming the usurpation, that the Pope *could give* authority to dispose of all ecclesiastical property.

But this doctrine was maintained as a part of the Supremacy from that time forward; and asserted even more explicitly afterwards : for Polemar, the Papal agent at the Council of Basle, (A. D. 1433) affirmed [m], that " *The Pope, as Vicar*

[1] Statuimus ut Ecclesiæ Romanæ legati—ex ipsius legationis munere conferendi beneficia nullam habeant potestatem, nisi hoc alicui specialiter, duxerimus indulgendum. Mansi, xxiii. c. 654.

[m] Papam, tanquam Christi Vicarium, qui universorum est Dominus, omnium civilium dominiorum esse primum administratorem, immo et Dominum, eo modo quo dominia hominibus sub Deo competunt. Canisii Thesaur. iv. p. 715. Compare the opinion of the Canonists, quoted by F. Rives; *All benefices in the world owe obedience in respect to the Pope*, (Omnia beneficia mundi sunt obedientialia respectu papalis potestatis) &c. Collier, Eccles. Hist. Records, ii. p. 107.

of Christ, who is Lord of all things, is chief admini-
strator, and even Lord, of all temporal domains, in
the same way in which domains belong to men under
God :" which, he said, might be proved from the
writings of many Doctors.

Pope Bonifacius VIII. exercised this power in a
different way, as if he meant to take the property
of the Church under his protection : for he by
the Bull "Clericis Laicos" inhibited the French
Clergy from paying any subsidy without permission from Rome[n].

Unlimited authority was claimed also over the
ministrations of the Clergy. The Popes could
command or prohibit from officiating, as they
liked. The Decrees of Rome on all subjects must
be obeyed by the Clergy.

Pope Nicolas II. in a Council at Rome (A. D.
1059) decreed, that no person should hear mass
from a married clerk, and that no married clerk
should say mass, or perform any office in the

---

[n] Mansi, xxiv. c. 1184. See the places referred to above
concerning this Pope's dispute with France.

Church, under pain of excommunication[o]. There were many married persons among the Clergy then, although marriage had been forbidden to them a few years before by a decree of Pope Leo IX. which Nicolas professed to follow up in his new Canon, all of whom would be ejected from their office at once by this law. Gregory VII, who was Nicolas' Archdeacon (Hildebrand) and chief adviser, renewed this Canon when he succeeded to the Papacy, and forbade the people from attending the ministrations of married Clergy in still stronger terms[p]. And it was repeated again afterwards, as at the second Lateran Council[q].

The interdicts, under which the Popes sometimes laid whole kingdoms, prove the same thing. By these all the sacred services of the Church were suspended throughout the nation. It was, in fact, a sentence of excommunication upon a district, to be executed by the Clergy.

[o] Mansi, xix. c. 897.
[p] Mansi, xx. c. 433. Matth. Paris, A. D. 1074. p. 7.
[q] Can. 6 and 7. Mansi, xxi. c. 527.

The interdict which Innocentius III. laid upon France, because Philip Augustus had forsaken his wife and unlawfully married another, A. D. 1199, may be taken for a specimen. It was in the following terms.

" Let all the Churches be shut, and let no one be admitted into them, except for the purpose of baptizing infants; and let them not be opened at all, except to light the candles, or when the priest shall fetch the Eucharist and holy water for the use of the sick. We suffer the mass to be celebrated once a week on Friday at daybreak, for a Eucharist for the use of the sick, one clerk only being allowed to enter to wait upon the priest. Let the priests preach on Sundays in the courts, and instead of the mass let them publish the Word of God. Let them say the canonical hours without the Churches, out of the hearing of the laity; if they say Epistle or Gospel, let them take care not to be overheard by the laity; and let them allow no body to be buried in the cemetery, under ground or above. Let them also tell the laity, that they

o

sin grievously and offend, if they even bury
bodies in the ground without the blessing, usurp-
ing in this matter the office of another. Let
them forbid their parishioners to enter the
Churches which are open in the King's lands.
Let them not bless the wallets of travellers,
except without the Churches. In Passion Week
let them not celebrate (mass), but defer it to
Easter Day; and then let them celebrate it in
private, no one being admitted, except one clerk,
as was said above; and let no one communicate
even at Easter, unless he be sick, and in danger
of death. In the same week, or on Palm Sunday,
let them give notice to the parishioners that
they may meet on the morning of Easter Day
before the Church, and permission will be given
them to eat flesh, [and] the holy bread of the
day. They are strictly forbidden to admit women
into the Church for purification : but let them
advise these to assemble their neighbours without the Church, and pray on the day of purification, and the women who were to be purified
shall not enter the Church, even to take away

from the holy font the infants who are to be baptized, until they are admitted by the priest after the interdict [is removed]. Let them hear confession of every one that asks for it in the Church porch: if the Church has no porch, then we suffer them to hear confessions at the threshold of the nearest door of the Church, which may be opened according to the severity of the weather, and not otherwise; all being shut out, except the person confessing, so that the priest and the person confessing may [not] be heard by those without the Church. But if the weather be fine, let confessions be heard before the closed doors of the Church. Let no vessels of holy water be set without the Church, nor the Clergy carry holy water, since all the sacraments of the Church, except those two aforesaid, are plainly prohibited. Extreme unction, which is a very great sacrament, must not be given [r]."

[r] Martene et Durand. Thesaur. Nov. Anecdot. iv. c. 147, and it is given in Mansi, xxii. c. 710. More specimens of interdict are to be seen in Ducange, Gloss. in v. [Conf. J. Hus. Op. i. p. 314. de Ecclesiâ.]

The interdict which the same Pope laid on England, A. D. 1208, was not revoked until A. D. 1214, after a large sum of money had been paid by the King for compensation to the Church: which sum it appears the Legate, who revoked the interdict, took good care to convey away with him out of the country untouched; desiring all who claimed a share of it, as compensation for their own losses, to carry their complaints to Rome, and seek redress there[s].

But the Supremacy did not stop with assuming power to control all the ministerial acts of all the Clergy. Still increasing in pretensions, it next grasped at the very existence of the ministry, and claimed to be itself *the source of all ministerial authority and spiritual office,* and *the dispenser of all sacramental grace to the Church.*

This was the doctrine of the Pope's advocate, Kalteisen, at the Council of Basle : " *Whatever of power, whatever of sacramental grace, whatever of heavenly dispensation, is given by Christ the Head of the Church, all this,* while the Church

[s] Matth. Paris, p. 209, 210.

is dispersed, and the Pope does not err in the faith, *is committed to his* (the Pope's) *dispensation*[t]." And again : "*Every election and institution to any rectory ought then* [in the time of the Apostles] *to have been* made *throughout the Church by S. Peter, and ever afterwards by his successors*[u] *:*" and, "*neither Bishops nor Priests may preach, unless sent specially by the Pope's authority.* For preaching is an act of jurisdiction :—but *all jurisdiction depends on the Pope*[x]." These positions Kalteisen maintained on the authority of many scholastic Doctors, referring often to the spurious writings which passed for those of Dionysius the Areopagite, and other forgeries

[t] "Quidquid enim potestatis, quidquid gratiæ sacramentalis, quidquid dispensationis cœlestis a Christo Capite Ecclesiæ commissum est, ipsa Ecclesia dispersa, et Papa in fide non errante, totum est ejus dispensationi commissum." Canisii Thesaur. iv. p. 632.   Compare also his argument on p. 646.

[u] "Omnis electio et institutio ad aliquam rectoriam pro tunc in tota Dei Ecclesia oportuit fieri a Petro, et deinceps ab ejus successore." Ibid. p. 650, from Hugutius.

[x] "Nec Episcopis nec Presbyteris liceat prædicare, nisi missis eis specialiter auctoritate Papæ.   Nam actus prædicationis est actus jurisdictionis, licet non coactivæ : sed omnis jurisdictio a Papa dependet." Ibid. p. 652, from Augustinus of Ancona.

under the name of Decretals of the early Popes. Among other things he put forward the monstrous assertion, that *all the Apostles received the power to execute their office of preaching, baptizing, and the like, from S. Peter* ʸ. Hence it followed, that S. Peter's successor alone can confer authority to minister in the Church of Christ.

And here I conclude my sketch of this wide subject. I have now traced in outline, as it were, the Papacy, noting down distinctly, though as shortly as possible, the critical changes and additions in it, the several steps by which it mounted, from the precedence which it originally possessed, to Supremacy ; a Supremacy which was not merely above all other power, but rather the absorption and concentration of all power in the world. For civil government was supposed

---

ʸ "Omnem ergo potestatem prædicandi, baptizandi, et similes, receperunt Apostoli a b. Petro post ascensionem Domini, non quoad auctoritatem, quia illam a Christo receperunt, sed quoad auctoritatis executionem, ne quis mitteret falcem in messem alienam spiritualiter aut temporaliter : unde ejus fuit diœceses dividere, unicuique suam assignare." Canisii Thesaur. iv. p. 650, from Cameracensis.

to be subject to it; and whatever authority existed in any part of the Church, was believed to be derived from the Pope, and virtually exercised by the Pope. It was a Pope who thus described the office; that he is "*the Vicar of Jesus Christ, the successor of Peter, the anointed of the Lord, the God of Pharaoh, short of God, beyond man, less than God, greater than man, who judges all men, and is judged by no man* z."

It has been shewn what the Papal Supremacy is, by the acts and declarations of Popes themselves, or their accredited agents. And these acts and declarations have been very different at different times. Few persons could give stronger testimony against that Supremacy, such as it has professed itself to be in later times, than the Popes of earlier ages would do, if we appealed to them. Indeed we might say, that the Popes continuously for ages tacitly *protested*, by that which

---

ᶻ "Vicarius Jesu Christi, successor Petri, Christus Domini, Deus Pharaonis, inter Deum et hominem medius constitutus, citra Deum, sed ultra hominem, minor Deo, sed major homine, qui de omnibus judicat, et a nemine judicatur." Innocent. III. Serm. 2. De Consecr. Pontif. p. 189. ed. Colon. 1575.

they omitted to do or to claim, against the ever-increasing claims and encroachments of their successors, who asserted powers so much beyond their own.

Two inferences therefore present themselves at this point for the consideration of those who allow the Supremacy.

First, they are bound to reconcile these differences in the history of the Papacy, and to shew that the principles and practices of the Popes in all ages agree in one consistent whole. Which they cannot do. It cannot be maintained with truth, that the principles which were asserted and acted upon by later Popes were contained virtually, and were *latent* in the Papacy of the earliest ages. Even if such a *mode* of argument were allowable on this question, (which it is not) it would not meet the case : because the difference is not that of *greater* and *less* only, nor of a *dormant title,* (which some might allege the authority of the Pope to have been in early ages) and a *claim asserted* as it was in later times; but it is a difference of *opposition.*

The Papacy of early times contradicts the assertions of the later Popes. Even the first Pope Gregory contradicted and condemned by anticipation the pretensions of the seventh Gregory. The extent of authority asserted, and the grounds on which it was claimed are contrary, we need not say to the doctrines of Scripture, the precepts of the Gospel, or to truth and justice, (for it is the historical view of the case which alone is considered here) but to all which history declares concerning the Bishopric of Rome from the earliest ages of the Church, whether we regard what the Bishops of early times considered to be their own due, or what the opinion and practice of the Church allowed to them.

When Pope Melchiades "*permitted*" (for it must have been done by *permission, if* the Pope were *supreme;* but he was not asked) the case of the Donatists, after it had been judged at Rome and a sentence given *by himself,* to be tried again the next year in a Council at Arles, by command of the Emperor, and on the petition of the parties, without any resistance on the part of the Pope, he plainly contradicted the doctrine of Pope Nicolas and others, that all jurisdiction is from Rome, that Councils "*meet only to hear the judgment of Rome.*"

When the Council of Nicæa made twenty Canons, these were received by the Church as of authority, because agreed to by a Council of the whole Church: and neither the Church, nor Pope Silvester, (who did *not* preside in the Council) nor any succeeding Pope for many ages, ever thought that the Canons "*would have no force, unless confirmed from S. Peter's Chair:*" thus the Church of the fourth century, and the Popes, contradicted Pope Gregory the Seventh.

When the Novatians denied that there was in the Church any authority to pronounce absolution upon penitents, we do not find that they were condemned for disputing the prerogative of S. Peter's successor over the Church. But they ought to have been condemned for this expressly, if the doctrine of Innocentius III. had been the doctrine of the Church then, viz. that *S. Peter and his successors, alone, can in the plenitude of their power remit all sins.*   Thus Pope Innocentius' assertion was implicitly denied in the third century.

Or when Pope Victor's too eager zeal against the Quartodeciman sect, by which he took upon himself to excommunicate them, was simply disregarded by the rest of the Church, and yet no great breach followed, no sending of Legates to read an Anathema, nor any attempt on the part of Rome to vindicate the authority of S. Peter's Chair over the whole Church, the Church of the second century plainly contradicted many fundamental positions of the later doctrine of the Supremacy, as to the necessity of being in communion with and obedience to S. Peter, and that S. Peter's Chair is the channel of all grace, order, and authority in the Church[a].

Such contrast and opposition between the early ages and later times are to be found through the whole history of the Papacy. Not one of those successive accretions of power, or "developments," which have been pointed out above as the stages

---

[a] [See what (Origen) says of Zephyrinus and Callistus. Refut. Hær. ix. 7, 11, &c. ed. Ox. 1851.]

by which the Supremacy arose, can be reconciled with the principles and the practice of the early ages. On the contrary, they were in general resisted when they first appeared.

So long as the Church was at liberty, the several acts of encroachment under the name of S. Peter met with continued opposition. The Churches of Greece, Asia, Syria, Africa, and even Britain, in turn *protested* against aggressions of various kinds.

When the Oriental and the African Churches were crushed by the Mahometan conquests, and the Roman Church had obtained complete ascendancy over all the West, those doctrines were propounded, as catholic truths, concerning S. Peter and his authority, on which the claim of the Supremacy as an Article of Religion is founded.

But these doctrines are irreconcilably opposed to the doctrines of the early Church. Either, therefore, they must be abandoned, because the evidence of history is all against them; or else the authority of antiquity and history must be given up, and those who hold them must confess, that they do not stand upon ancient usage and the consent of the primitive Church; but that the distinguishing principle and chief Article of their system is of later growth.

Secondly, although in this review we have seen the Supremacy in various stages of growth, it is in the last stage that it appears with that form under which it would *now* claim authority. Since each succeeding act by which it advanced, and each new assertion of power, when made, had (as it was pretended) a distinct divine authority over the consciences of men, by virtue of the commission given to S. Peter and his successors, since *nothing has ever been revoked*, i. e. no Papal claim *once made ever renounced and condemned as untrue or unfounded by later Popes*, it follows that the Supremacy *which now is*, and which asserts its own right over the Church, requiring universal submission to the Vicar of Christ, is the aggregate of all the powers which have ·been heretofore asserted or exercised by Popes at any time. Men may read the history of the See of Rome, and exercise judgment on the acts of Popes, as an amusement, perhaps; and perhaps by some inevitable impulse of nature be driven to sympathize rather with a martyred Cornelius, or a Julius contending for the faith, than with a triumphant Pope Innocentius III. or Gregory IX; but it is the latest and broadest development only which can be acknowledged to be the *true, divinely-constituted Supremacy,* by those who receive it. For whatever it has declared itself to be, such on its own principles it must be, by the word of "*infallible*" truth.

The characters of the Supremacy of the thirteenth and fourteenth centuries are stereotyped by Papal infallibility. The Legate of the Pope at the Diet of Ratisbon, A. D. 1541, asserted, that *infallibility is the personal privilege of the Pope, given by the words of our Lord, spoken to S. Peter,* "Peter, I have prayed for thee [b]."

And subsequent acts of the Papacy give no indication of greater liberty, in regard to the Supremacy. The Council of Trent carefully pro-

---

[b] P. Sarpi, Hist. du Conc. de Trente, v. i. p. 171. ed. Couray.

vided for the rigorous enforcing of obedience to the Pope, and the profession of entire belief in his divine Supremacy.

The Bull of Pope Pius IV. entitled, " On the Form of Oath of Profession of the Faith," contains a Profession of Faith which all who are appointed to any benefice or office in the Church are required to swear to: in it is the following passage [c]: " The holy Catholic and Apostolic Roman Church I acknowledge to be *the mother and mistress of all Churches:* and I promise and swear *true obedience* to the Roman Pontiff, the successor of *S.Peter, the Prince of the Apostles, and Vicar of Jesus Christ.* Also I profess and *receive without any doubt all the other* things delivered, defined, and declared by the holy *Canons and General Councils,* and especially by the *most holy Synod of Trent."* The

---

[c] " Sanctam Catholicam et Apostolicam Romanam ecclesiam omnium ecclesiarum matrem et magistram agnosco : Romanoque pontifici beati Petri Apostolorum principis successori, ac Jesu Christi vicario veram obedientiam spondeo ac juro. Cætera item omnia a sacris canonibus et œcumenicis conciliis, ac præcipue a sacrosancta Tridentina synodo tradita, definita, et declarata, in-dubitanter recipio et profiteor." Can. et Decr. Conc. Trid.

Council of Trent had decreed much to the same effect in Sess. xxv. De Reform. c. 2.

And with regard to the Pope's authority, it was expressly provided, that nothing ordered in that Council should affect it[d].

It would seem therefore that nothing that has ever been done by Papal authority can be called in question by those who hold the doctrine of the "Supremacy." Although a man held everything else which the Roman Communion teaches, yet if he doubted, *that Popes can depose Princes from their thrones, and release subjects from their obedience ;* or that *the Pope by his plenary power can remit all sins ;* or that *all the Councils of the Church have, and can have, authority only from the Pope's confirmation ;* or that *all Bishops and Clergy have mission and power to minister by the authority of the Pope alone ;* or that *all heretics are to be extirpated by the secular power ;* or that *all the property of the Church belongs to the Pope, so that*

---

[d] " *Ut in his salva semper auctoritas sedis Apostolicæ et sit et esse intelligatur.*" Can. et Decr. Conc. Trid. Sess. xxv. De Reform. c. 21.

he can dispose of it as he will; or that *all juris-diction in the Church proceeds from the Pope,* so that *all ecclesiastical causes,* whether in China, America, Ethiopia, or Siberia, *must be carried to Rome for final settlement;*—if he doubted any of these, or many similar positions, he must, on these principles, offend against the great duty of obedience to S. Peter's successors: and it seems to follow, that he could not be tolerated, nor have the promise of salvation in the Roman Communion.

This then, it appears, in conclusion, is the doctrine of the *Supremacy* of the Pope. It must be received *undoubted,* and *entire,* such as the Popes have declared it, and acted upon it. To attempt to qualify or modify it, is to deny the authority of it altogether. If it be anything less than it has asserted itself to be, unless (such as it has asserted itself to be) it be *in everything* the divine ordinance of our blessed Lord and Saviour, it is false, a fiction, and an imposture.

www.ingramcontent.com/pod-product-compliance
Lightning Source LLC
Chambersburg PA
CBHW031419020726
47499CB00005B/1506